The C.O.R.E. Principles

The C.O.R.E. Principles

ASAT™ C.O.R.E. Counseling
and the Pursuit of Becoming More

Martin Hart

ASAT Press
Topsfield, Massachusetts

Published by ASAT Press

Designed by creativepublishingdesign.com

Copyright © Martin Hart 2020

All rights reserved. No part of this publication may be reproduced, stored in a retrieval system, or transmitted in any form or by any means, electric, mechanical, photocopying, recording or otherwise, without the prior permission of the copyright owner.

For press and media related inquiries, contact: Martin Hart, asat@asat.org

Paperback / Softcover ISBN: 9780989551854
eBook ISBN: 9780989551861

Library of Congress Control Number: 2020917423

Copies are available at special rates for bulk orders. Contact the sales team at ASAT Press, asat@asat.org

For My Clients and Students

What an Adventure! What a Ride!

Table of Contents

Introduction 1

Part 1
How Things Come to Be

01: The Importance of Knowing Where to Look 7
    The Frog and the Bubble 9
    The Movie on the Screen 11

02: Make Believe: You Make It Then Believe It 15
    "The Play's the Thing" 19

03: If a Tree Falls in a Forest 21

04: How to Heal a Boson and a Fermion 27
    Navigating the Gap 30

05: The Basic Components of Reality Creation 33
    The Raw Materials 34
    The Tools 35
    The Skills 37

06: The Basic Components of Self-Change 41
    Attend to the Whispers and the Shouts 45
    Process and Program 46
    Use Technique 47
    Be Willing and Allowing 48

07: Beyond Curing, Beyond Fixing 51
    The Laws of Evolution: The Growth of Thoughts and Forms 54
    Ending Destructive Thoughts and Ideas 55

Part 2
Following the C.O.R.E. Map Home

08: So, What's Up? 61
   The Conscious, Subconscious, and Unconscious 63
   The Law of Action and Reaction 65

09: The C.O.R.E. Map to Self-Healing 67

10: (C)onscious 73

11: (O)wnership 79
   Payoffs 80
   The 'R' Word 82

12: (R)elease 87
   The Power of Forgiveness 89

13: (E)ngage 93

14: Parts Therapy: Healing the Whole of You 97
   Attending to Your Developing Selves 100
   The Dark Counselors 103
   Essential Points to Consider When Working With Your Developing Selves and Dark Counselors 107

15: Growing Your Spirituality 113
   Your Future Self 117
   Your Higher Self 118
   Your Soul and Spirit 119
   God, Goddess, All That Is 120

16: The Golf Course and the River 121
   The Sacred Hallows 124

Part 3
How C.O.R.E Counseling Works

17: ASAT C.O.R.E. Counseling 131
   Notes for the C.O.R.E. Counselor 134

18: The 4 Ds.. 139
    Denial 142
    Discounting.. 142
    Distraction... 143
    Defense 143

19: Three Clients... 145
    The Get-bys 146
    The Move ons.. 147
    The Move Beyonds 148

20: The Hidden Killers 153

21: Round Trip from Eden: Beyond Healing 163
    The Sacred Covenant: Coming Home 164
    Becoming More... 167

Appendix One
Questions and Answers

Appendix Two
Techniques

Appendix Three
Glossary

Appendix Four
The American Society of Alternative Therapists (ASAT)

Appendix Five
ASAT Training Courses

About the Author

Introduction

Some strive to become a better version of themselves. Some strive to become perfect, an impossible undertaking, and some are satisfied with simply fixing a broken life. Some toil and struggle to accumulate more things in their limited view of success and happiness, while others are merely content to pass the time while waiting to die. But there are a few, not many, who desire to become more: not perfect, not better, not fixed, not merely having more, and not wanting to waste a perfectly good life. These few are destined to succeed in their quest, for becoming more is, in truth, the destiny of all. And what's destined to be will inevitably happen in time and in accordance with one's choosing. ASAT™ C.O.R.E. Counseling, and this book *The C.O.R.E principles*, are intended for people such as these.

C.O.R.E. is an acronym for conscious, ownership, release, and engage. It's not a philosophy or a philosophical system or a healing modality or a series of alternative techniques and approaches; it's a map and a guide for those willing and determined to consciously create a successful and rewarding life, filled with elegance and magical synchronicities. For those seeking to reclaim the authorship of their lives, C.O.R.E can be a guide. And for those choosing to journey on a road of ever-unfolding self-awakening, C.O.R.E. can serve as a map. But C.O.R.E. is not for everyone; it's only for the few who choose to travel a different path, a path of Coming Home.

The first certification class of ASAT™ C.O.R.E. counselors began in January 1990. For the next thirty years, hundreds of practitioners, along with thousands of their clients, journeyed their destined paths of growth and self-awakening with the guidance of the C.O.R.E map. At times their journey took them down bumpy and challenging roads; at times, the way forward was smooth and frictionless. At times their journey took them deep into dark and frightening places, at times to places of unimaginable beauty and enchantment. All were map-makers to virgin futures, all were crafters of more vibrant, more fulfilling lives, and each a participant in a grand adventure of becoming more.

Through the efficacy of ASAT™ C.O.R.E. Counseling, my fellow counselors and I have witnessed and are still witnessing the lives of our clients' grow and thrive in remarkable ways. They're crafting extraordinary realities, rich in fun, accomplishment, and magic. Where struggle and conflict once existed, adventure and elegance now flourish, and all this unfolds in a remarkably short time. They report being happier, healthier, and more successful, and their lives magically overflow with remarkable synchronicities. It's inspiring to hear and glorious to behold.

Over the years, I've been asked by students and clients to write a book about C.O.R.E.; I tried many times to do so but with little success. Whenever I'd get about halfway, C.O.R.E. would change, and I'd have to start all over. Every time I thought I finally got a handle on it, C.O.R.E. would evolve and take on a new and different shape and texture. C.O.R.E. is an elusive lover, always seductive, always teasing, and always just beyond my reach. But I realized, over time, that it would always be that way, and it would always need to be. For C.O.R.E. was more than some counseling approach, some alternative facilitation method, or some series of healing modalities; it was a vibrant and living thing.

All living things grow and evolve and become stronger, and C.O.R.E. was doing precisely that. So, I finally gave up fighting and decided to write of its essence, its heart, and its inherent realness. I chose not to write about C.O.R.E. but to allow C.O.R.E. to write about itself. The process now became more natural, more fluid, and more fulfilling. And thirty years later, this book, The *C.O.R.E Principles,* came to be written.

The C.O.R.E. Principles is an introduction to a process rich in complexity and ripe with challenges requiring honest response and participation; it's a guidebook for those seeking a different approach to healing and self-mastery. And it was written for the few who wish to pursue more magic, more authorship, and more conscious awareness in their lives. It's for those willing to respond to life, not react to it.

The C.O.R.E. Principles contains three sections. Part 1 explores the foundations of reality creating. It provides a basis for understanding how everything in creation comes into manifestation, our place in that manifesting process, and how we shape and sustain what we create, and, more importantly, how we can elevate and even transcend all we create and experience. Part 2 explores the C.O.R.E. process: what it is, how it works, how it guides and maps our unique journey of becoming more. Part 3 covers the counseling practice and the ways and means of implementing the C.O.R.E. map to affect the change we seek and monitor the challenges and the resistance we'll experience along the way.

This book is written for both counselors and those seeking the knowledge and the means to advance their life consciously and more elegantly. The book will serve both counselor and seeker as a guide to self-healing and self-discovery. It will provide insights, tools, and techniques for crafting a more fulfilling, more successful, and more rewarding life.

A journey lies before you, a journey complete with challenges, not struggles, consciously created opportunities, not a life lived at the whims of fate or luck, and grand adventures, not a life of toil and crisis like so many others choose to live. A life of becoming more awaits you. If such a life is for you, read on.

Enjoy!

PART 1
How Things Come to Be

CHAPTER 1

The Importance of Knowing Where to Look

Heal at the source. Stop nibbling at its fringes.
Melt the icebergs that rise before you.
Stop navigating your ship around them.
This way, your voyage will become more elegant.

A man is standing beneath a street lamp, one dark evening, looking for something on the ground. A stranger walks by, notices the man, and asks, "Did you lose something, Sir?"

"Yes, I lost my car keys," the man replies.

The kind stranger immediately offers to help find the lost keys.

After looking for some time with no result, the stranger, frustrated but wanting to be helpful, says, "Are you sure you lost the keys here?"

"Oh, no!" said the man. "I lost them over there in the shadows by the wall."

"Then why are we looking here?" asks the stunned stranger.

"Because there's more light." Replies the man.

Like the man looking needlessly in well-lit places for keys he knows are lying in dark shadows, we'll never find healing if we do not exercise the will and courage to search the dark places we fear to go. We can cure, that's true, but curing is not the same as healing. Healing requires knowledge of where to look and the willingness to delve deep into the hidden and often fearsome places within us.

The terms "curing" and "healing" are often misunderstood and often erroneously interchanged. For many, they refer to the same thing. Although both have as their objective the elimination of a problem or a condition, be it physical, mental, emotional, or spiritual, what it means to heal something is vastly different from what it means to cure it. While curing ends the problem or condition, healing addresses its foundation, thus ending the need for its return. Healing works beyond space and time and depth. The differences are dimensional.

Curing is temporary, healing permanent. Although curing occurs instantaneously, it unfolds over time. Healing, likewise, occurs instantaneously and similarly plays out over time, but since healing transcends space and time, it alters space and time; it changes our very condition. Curing fixes us; healing changes us.

For example, if I have a problem with mosquitoes, I can spray the pond and kill the mosquito larvae. This spraying will fix, will cure, the problem, but the pond, the breeding ground for the mosquitoes, remains. The mosquitoes will lay eggs again, and ultimately return. But if I drain the pond, if I heal the pond, thus destroying the breeding ground, the problem will be gone; no more mosquitoes.

Health practitioners may claim to heal, but, in truth, most don't. That doesn't take away from the importance of their valuable work of curing, but healing is not what they do. They can end the problem, but the pond remains; the breeding ground still lingers. Healing is required to correct the problem ultimately.

The Frog and the Bubble

There lives beneath the sand at the bottom of a pond, a frog. One day the frog burps. As a result, a bubble forms. As the bubble rises to the surface, it grows bigger and bigger. In time we notice the bubble at the pond's surface. We decide to get rid of the bubble by popping it. In doing so, we've eliminated the presence of the bubble; we've cured the bubble problem. But the bubble did not originate at the surface; it did not originate from the first bubble; it originated as distress within the frog living unnoticed beneath the sand. Addressing the bubble anywhere other than within the frog is valuable, but it's not healing.

To use another example, a doctor discovers a defective heart valve in his patient. The doctor surgically replaces the malfunctioning valve resulting in the patient living an active and healthy life. The doctor cured him, but he did not heal him. The source of the problem remains unaddressed. As stated earlier, this in no way diminishes the value and importance of the doctor's work.

Addressing the heart condition, and the bubble, when we catch it at the surface of the pond, is of the utmost importance. But, it's not healing. Remember, the bubble originated within the frog. We experience the bubble when it surfaces in the same way we experience the heart condition through symptoms or detection in some other way. Unless dealt with at its source, the bubble will emerge again in a similar or different form. It will surface because it's not healed. A hidden, unaddressed issue will always demand our attention in one form or another.

The bubble always comes to the surface, never the other way around. The problem is not the bubble; the problem is the frog's distress. All life's many issues, illnesses, and crises originate within the Unconscious. In time and space, it will become conscious to us physically, emotionally, or through other problems and conditions. In time, it will surface in the guise of fate.

Where to look? Where to heal the distress?

Look to the Unconscious, for all illness and suffering have their source there. What lies hidden deep within the Unconscious, what we store there, must, in time, surface. We must come face to face with what we've locked away so we can consciously address it. This surfacing must occur. Our healing requires it.

A malfunctioning heart valve is a bubble we experience, it's the form a particular issue has taken, but the issue's origin is within the Unconscious. It's there we pursue its ultimate healing. The many factors leading to the faulty valve, such as poor diet, stress, genetic or environmental influences, etc. are the emerging bubbles rising to the surface. Each bubble has a more significant impact, the closer it comes to the top. We experience the bubble at the surface, but often ignore it as it rises from the frog. Curing, and even preventing the condition on a short term basis, requires we pay attention.

Everything resides within the Unconscious. Our outer world is a part of the Unconscious we make real for ourselves consciously. It's an out-picturing of our inner, hidden world. We use measuring devices to make the Unconscious real for us: our five senses, our beliefs and attitudes, thoughts and feelings, choices and decisions, our temporal lobes, our subconscious projections, etc.

The Movie on the Screen

Think of our reality as a movie projected on a blank screen. The story's not real; it's an illusion we make real through our suspension of disbelief. We're the ones who write, produce, cast, and place the film before the projector of our attention. Change the movie, re-write the script, and we alter what we observe and experience; we alter what we give attention to. Trying to change the film on the level of the screen is pointless. The images on the screen are not real, but the story projected is the reality we're choosing to observe and live. It's real to us because we believe it is, and because we give it meaning, value, and attention.

How do we heal, then? Do we go into the Unconscious somehow to discover what's there? You could, but you wouldn't remember what you've found; you're unconscious. There are, however, two ways to discover what the Unconscious is telling you, what it needs you to address:

(1) We could wait, knowing that whatever lies within our unconscious, will in time, become conscious in the form of fate, or, in other words, when the bubble reaches the surface. This method, though most elect to take this route, is not recommended.

(2) We can respond to its messages. We can pay attention to how the Unconscious speaks to us, we can pay attention to the emerging bubbles, and we can learn to understand its language and choose to act upon what we've learned. We can become conscious of our reality's many whispers and shouts. I recommend this route.

The language of the Unconscious is not linear. It does not speak in English, French, Latin, or Urdu. It speaks in the non-linear language of myth, metaphor, archetype, and symbol. When we step back and observe our reality as a myth, a metaphor, an archetypal reflection, or a symbol, we gain a greater sense of what the Unconscious is trying to communicate.

When we step back from the movie, when we end our suspension of disbelief, when we accept that we're its author, then we have the power to change it.

In linear language, 'heart' is a specific organ of the body. In the language of the Unconscious, 'heart,' being a symbol of love, can express any issue concerning love: self-love, love's loss and pain, love's absence, love's humiliation, love's betrayal, a sense of abandonment, etc. When made conscious in our reality, issues of the heart can manifest at the surface of the pond as physical conditions or relationship problems, or in any area related to the emotional heart. Address the Unconscious issue, and there's no need for its physical manifestation. Bubbles will not surface if we heal the frog's distress. But the Unconscious must be addressed consciously for such healing to occur.

In linear language, 'blood' refers to *"the fluid that circulates in the heart, arteries, capillaries, and veins that carry nourishment and oxygen to, and brings away waste from, all parts of the body"* (Merriam Webster Dictionary). High blood pressure, leukemia, or any health issue involving blood, is the surfaced bubble. It's our unconscious shout to address a more deep-rooted problem needing immediate attention. Blood is often a metaphor for family or familial connections. Perhaps the need is to attend to deeper issues around blood ties such as family, community, the nurturing of loved ones or lack thereof, our sense of disconnection, etc.

Remember, whatever lies within the Unconscious will, in time, become conscious in the form of fate. Whatever distress is present within the frog must emerge and grow until it appears full-blown at the pond's surface.

The Unconscious is not punishing us; it's attempting to get our attention. It's trying to help us. It's trying to get us to address a hidden problem that stands between us and living a life of health, happiness, and freedom. Everything in our reality is there to help us become more. Nothing in our reality is there to harm us unless we create, or allow it so. We may not have created the malfunctioning heart valve, the cancer, or the heart attack, but we allowed it by not listening to the whispers before they became shouts.

When we pay attention to our unconscious whispers, when we learn to listen and observe our reality with sharpened and honed measuring devices, we can transcend anything, we can heal anything. We can turn a tragedy into a love story, a melodrama into a comedy. We can re-write the story in the projector of our conscious perception.

Like the lost car keys, true healing, as well as discovering the more real in us, require that we look in the darkest shadows of ourselves. Healing awaits us there; treasures beyond what we can imagine await us there.

CHAPTER 2

Make Believe: You Make It Then Believe It

Your life is a story of your own creation.
If you don't like the story, rewrite it.
If you like the story, make it better.
You're here to author a masterpiece.

Over ninety years ago, quantum physicists demonstrated that all matter is, in fact, not matter at all, but a wave. And they found that when attention is given to a wave, it collapses into a particle, thus creating a form; matter. When the ancients described all reality as an illusion, they were stating a truth modern science proved thousands of years later to be true. The 'single slot' and 'double slot' experiments are two notable examples showing the emergence of a particle from a wave by the simple act of attention.

In the single slot experiment, researchers took a box and placed a tiny hole on opposite sides. Inside the box, they lined the walls with a photo-like filament that would record tracings, or footprints, when anything interacted with it. They then shot a photon particle of light through one of the holes. What emerged from the opening on the opposite side was a particle of light. However, what amazed the researchers, was when they opened the box, they found tracings along the filament lined walls of the box indicating the movement of a wave. The particle, in the box and away from the attention of the observer, reverted to its natural wave state. When it emerged from the hole on the opposite side, the wave collapsed once again into a particle. The researchers concluded that this 'collapsing' was due to the attention given to it.

In the double slot experiment, researchers made a box with two tiny holes in one side and a single hole in the opposite. This time, when the photon was shot through the single hole, it emerged as two distinct particles, one from each hole at the opposite side. What makes this so remarkable is that you cannot divide a photon into two separate particles. Where did the second photon come from? The scientists concluded that it came into being from the attention, and intention, given by the observers, the scientists themselves. In other words, the wave responded by collapsing into two particles due not only to the attention given by the observers but by the observer's intention for two particles to emerge. And during other similar experiments, the photon not only responded to the observer's intentions but anticipated them. Now, what can we conclude from this?

All reality is a wave (illusion) made real (form) based on the attention, and intention, given it.

To summarize, everything is, in essence, a wave. A wave becomes form when given attention and intention. What we intend something to be, whether we're conscious of it or not, will determine what we perceive and thus give attention to, and, as a result, what we experience as form, or what we call reality. But what we call reality is, in truth, an illusion we make-believe is real.

You're sitting in a room. Everything outside this room, everything outside your experience, is, in fact, a wave. Only when you give attention does the wave become real to you because you collapsed the wave into a particle. When you sleep at night, everything, including yourself, is in its natural state, a wave. You're not conscious; you're unconscious. You're not giving attention to anything; therefore, everything reverts to its natural state, a wave. Your dreams are not in particle form; they're information emerging from your unconscious, filtered through the templates of your subconscious, to create the stories you experience while sleeping. When you wake, the wave becomes form once again because you now give it attention.

"But wait! My wife reading next to me is still form, isn't she?"

To you, no, but to her, yes, because she's conscious and giving attention to herself and the room, and everything else around her. For you, however, she's no longer a form; she's a more real non-dimensional wave. Because you're asleep and are not giving her attention, you're not collapsing the wave into particle.

A wave is real. A particle, our perceived reality, is not. Again, as the ancients once taught, our reality is an illusion, a dream we make real so we can interact with it.

Our reality is a make-believe story. We make it by collapsing the wave, and then believe the story to be true in form. And since we give our reality value and meaning, it makes it more real for us. In this way, we, as a consciousness perceived as a three-dimensional form, can exist in a perceived three-dimensional illusion we call reality.

To make reality real for us, we need materials from which to craft that reality. These materials consist of our beliefs and attitudes, thoughts and feelings, choices and decisions. Everything in existence is glued together by these components. To change your reality, we must change these components.

Your reality is a story you convince yourself is real. The story is not real, but you believe it is; it's called "make-believe."

Nothing in your reality is what you think it is. You give it belief in accordance to what you give attention to, and the intention and meaning you give it. If your story is a victim's story, the reality you experience will be a victim's reality. You're not, in truth, a victim, but with your attention on victimhood, and with the intentions you're giving it, and the meaning and value, or weight, it holds for you, you make it so. Change the story, and you change your reality. But to do this, you must change the attention you give to it, the intentions underlying it, and the meaning and value, or weight, it holds for you. You will also need to change the beliefs and attitudes, thoughts and feelings, and choices and decisions you're still holding onto that attract that victim story.

In working the C.O.R.E. map, the therapist needs to be aware that whatever the client is saying is just a story the client is making real for his or her self, nothing more. The therapist must always challenge the client's story. The story's not real; it's make-believe. If the therapist buys into the story, the therapist is enabling it; the therapist is legitimizing the illusion. The issue is the 'why' behind the story, not the story itself. Change the story by addressing the 'why' of it. Change the 'why' of the story, and you can rewrite it. The therapist must always focus on and challenge where the client gives attention, intention, meaning, and value.

The Play's the Thing

Shakespeare's *Hamlet* is a story. It's not real. If you're living the *Hamlet* story, attend to the *Hamlet* within you. It's from that secret place within you that you give attention, intention, and meaning and value to the story. Once addressed and healed by addressing why you're doing it, you can write a different story, maybe a love story or a tale of adventure or both. You're Shakespeare; *Hamlet* is your play. The reality you experience will always be a story written by what you give attention to, the intentions behind it, and the weight of the meaning and value you give it. You're making it, and you believe it's true. Again, this is make-believe.

You have a destiny. And that destiny is to live a story that will, over time, reflect more of the real you, the very essence of the magnificence of you. But first, you'll need to be conscious of the current story you've convinced yourself is real. You'll need to own the story by acknowledging it and by attending to why you're doing it. You'll need to choose to let the old story go and exercise the courage to do so. And you'll need to forgive yourself for having held onto it. When you do these things, engage in a different story, one more reflective of the truer you.

Learning to create our reality consciously is the real purpose of our life. Our life's goal should always involve becoming more with elegance and grace, fun and adventure, and abundance and bountiful living. We're all destined for this calling. Living a life of freedom, becoming the Being of Light we are, and always expanding to become more should be our life's purpose, but, as always, it's our call to pursue it or not.

So, what's your story? What do you believe is real? What wave are you collapsing into form? And why are you creating it, believing it, and doing it?

CHAPTER 3

If a Tree Falls in a Forest

*You have the power and authority
to change everything in your reality.
Claim that power and authority
and use it to elevate yourself,
for nothing changes until you do.*

Question:

If a tree falls in the forest, and there's no one there to hear it, does it make a sound?

Answer:

There's no tree.

Life's an illusion. This understanding is arguably among the oldest truths held by humankind. For thousands of years, traditions in the East, and more recently in the West, proclaimed this truth. From hymns chanted by Vedic pundits and Buddhist monks, extolling the transient nature of reality (Maya) to the inspired writings of Western Transcendentalists seeking the eternal, immutable realness found in the beauty and enchantment of Nature, poets, philosophers, visionaries, and seekers cognized this ancient truth. Deep within the inner recesses of the human heart, all seek realness. Deep within our yearning Soul, all seek the eternal beyond the finite illusions we call reality and becoming one with God/Goddess/All That Is lies at the bases of all our actions and pursuits, benevolent or otherwise.

Our reality is an illusion made real by us, the observer. The tree appears from its essence (wave) only when there's an observer present to collapse the wave into form (particle) through the process of attention. For hundreds of years, we've convinced ourselves that Newton's Law of Cause and Effect is how reality comes into being. Like Newton, we were wrong. All we observe comes into being through what scientists now term "resonance causation."

Everything is, in essence, a wave, a frequency of vibration. The innumerable frequencies that makeup waves range from lowest to highest. When two or more waves meet, an independent wave called a "standing wave" emerges out of the interaction. This standing wave is also referred to as a "grand attractor" as it attracts other waves to it. This grand attractor will draw higher or lower resonances depending on the frequency that's closest to its own. As a synergy, this independent wave is always greater than the sum of its parts.

When an observer engages with a particular resonance, or in other words, when the observer gives attention to it, one of three things will occur; the higher wave will lower, the lower will rise, or they'll meet somewhere in-between. This process is the "Law of Resonance." If the higher wave elevates the lower, the standing wave will attract higher frequencies; if the lower wave diminishes the higher wave, the standing wave will attract lower frequencies. If both waves meet somewhere in between, the standing wave attracts compromised frequencies. There's only one acceptable outcome, and that's to elevate lower frequencies. Compromise is never a good idea because compromise always involves lowering a higher resonance.

Whatever we give attention to, we engage in a resonance interaction with it. For example, when two or more people interact, out of this interaction, a synergy is formed called a "relationship." This relationship, this grand attractor, will draw other waves to it, realities reflective of the relationship. This interaction, this relationship, this synergy, will lower the participants, elevate them, or they'll compromise somewhere in between.

All thoughts and feelings, beliefs and attitudes, choices and decisions are waves; are resonances. By engaging with them, we participate in a resonance interaction with them. For example, if we give attention to the belief that we're unloved and unappreciated, in other words, we're being martyred; one of three outcomes will result. We'll lower our resonance to the lower frequency of martyrhood, or we'll lift its frequency, thus healing it, or we'll compromise with it.

Healing involves giving attention to what we hold within ourselves and choosing and taking action to lift its resonance. If we engage in martyrhood, healing requires we raise its frequency.

The elevated resonance of martyr is magic. Therefore we can lower ourselves to a martyred reality or compromise with it or elevate ourselves to a magical reality; all that's required is that we give attention to what we're creating and make a choice and take steps to lift it. But the key is to engage by giving it attention. Just saying the words does not alter its resonance. As two or more waves must meet to form a resonance interaction, one must face the components of one's current reality head-on: not run from it and wish for the best, or compromise with it, or take half measures.

With the Law of Resonance, we know that when two or more waves meet, an independent wave emerges from the interaction. The interaction does not create this wave; the wave appears. It's a synergy greater than the sum of its parts. The standing wave is real; what's attracted to it is an illusion.

Whatever you store deep within yourself has already involved your interaction with it; you've already engaged in resonance causation with it. Although it's not conscious to you, it's experienced in your reality because your reality is simply an out-picturing of what you've made real within yourself, what you've pushed into your unconscious. The resonances within you and their standing wave attractors are what attract like energies into your experience that gives your reality the form that reflects those inner realities. What lies within your unconscious is real; what your conscious mind perceives is not; it's only a reflection; it's only a story you convince yourself is real.

Healing requires that we enter the hidden places within ourselves and face the demons we store there. These demons, these energies, though well hidden, are none-the-less made real to us by the act of avoidance and harboring. Every belief and attitude we hold is an act of resonance engagement; likewise, every thought and feeling we have and every choice and decision we make. Changing our reality, not merely fixing it, requires we give attention to all we create or allow, and by way of that attention, lift the resonances we're engaging consciously or unconsciously. Healing requires we elevate the synergy, not lower or compromise with it. Changing our reality requires we change from the very source of that reality; ourselves. As the saying goes, *"Nothing changes until you do."*

C.O.R.E. never wastes time and attention by attempting to correct illusions. C.O.R.E. focuses on changing reality by changing it at the source of the projection; you. The story playing out on the screen of our attention is not real; its origin is the story's author. Re-write the script, change the film, and the story becomes different. However, the story cannot change until the author chooses and takes action to change it. Healing, transforming one's story, must always begin and end with the story's creator.

Does a tree make a noise if it falls in a forest?

Only if you create or allow it so

CHAPTER 4

How to Heal a Boson and a Fermion

Life ebbs and flows.
There'll be times when you must flow (act)
and times when you must ebb (reflect).
Honor both.

Bosons and fermions are two classes of sub-atomic particles; bosons named after the Indian physicist and Nobel Laureate Satyendra Nath Bose, fermions after Italian physicist and Nobel Laureate Enrico Fermi. Both particles are opposite in their make-up and behavior. Fermions are highly volatile, while bosons are stable and more coherent. However, when placed in a steadily lowering temperature, both particles display similar behaviors.

Scientists studied both particles to see how they would react when applying the Third Law of Thermodynamics. According to the law, as the temperature lowers to a state of absolute zero (-273.15c), the lowest possible temperature where nothing can be colder and no heat remains in a substance, entropy (disorder) decreases while order increases. With decreasing temperature, the chaotic nature of fermions became less chaotic and more coherent; the same applied to bosons, although bosons are by their nature, more coherent. However, when both particles reached the gap between -273.14c and -273.15c, all hell broke loose. Both bosons and fermions went bonkers. They went into a state of pure chaotic frenzy. But when they emerged from the gap, both particles became completely different. They were now quantum mechanical, super symmetrical, infinitely coherent, and completely stable and transcendent. They became what particle physicists call "Super-Particles." Bosons and fermions were not changed, were not fixed, were not cured, and were not healed; they were different particles. Bosons and fermions transcended the need for curing and healing; they were now super functioning. By becoming new, not fixed, or changed, they achieved the ultimate goal of healing, a state of Oneness, and infinite coherence.

Scientists refer to this gap as a "phase transition." Within this gap is a state of complete chaos.

Chaos precedes all significant change, and chaos is essential to transcendence. How we navigate this gap, this chaos, will determine whether our journey to the ultimate of healing,

Oneness, will be fraught with mounting crisis, or characterized by a life lived in elegance and synchronicity. The goal remains the same; only the journey is different from one individual to another depending on their relationship with chaos.

Curing is essential, but a state of Oneness is the ultimate goal. Healing is how we get there. Curing and healing both involve what's commonly referred to as a "healing crisis," but healing stands alone in the range and magnitude of the experience, the chaos encountered; for the greater the change, the greater the disorder preceding it.

This 'gap,' with its frenzy, lack of predictability, and uncontrollability, is why most settle for curing and shun the pursuit of healing. Most will never invade the dark hidden places within themselves necessary to affect the healing. Never-the-less, this is the goal of ASAT™ C.O.R.E. Counseling, and this is the challenge of the ASAT™ C.O.R.E. counselor.

Each of us is on a magnificent journey of becoming more with the ultimate pursuit of a life lived in Oneness. Each of us will undertake this journey differently, some through pain and struggle, some through lightness and elegance; it's all a function of one's choice and attention. All goals are ultimately the same, but not so the means of getting there. This is not to imply that one approach is better than another, but it does suggest that the infinite ways of getting there range from the depths of struggle and misery to the heights of joy and bounteous living. The goal is what's important; we can get there crying and weeping or laughing and singing. It's your choice.

Navigating the Gap

We're all in the process of significant evolutionary change; we're all becoming multi-dimensional. All change is preceded by chaos; the more significant the change, the more significant the chaos. Our evolution from a three-dimensional to a multi-dimensional reality will, by its very magnitude, contain immense periods of turmoil and upheaval. These conditions are essential parts of this growing process. Such times are not punishments and are not judgments on our value and worth. We've chosen this journey we're on, and we've accepted the conditions necessary to achieve our desired goal of becoming more. But our journey doesn't have to be as difficult and as bumpy as we're making it. We can make different choices, and we can elect to have more elegant and more synchronous experiences. We can weather our times of chaos with dignity and grace, and we can rise to grander heights by navigating them with panache and mastery.

Navigating our times of chaos is a skill worth cultivating and an undertaking worth pursuing. Such navigating involves four steps.

Understanding: When we find ourselves in the gap, in the chaos, don't get swept up in the frenzy and turmoil of such chaotic times. Pause, reflect, and understand this place in which we find ourselves. Recognize the chaos as a necessary part of our way forward and choose to proceed with elegance and courage. Understanding our journey, our path, is essential for self-mastery and more elegant and straightforward navigation.

Acceptance: Welcome the chaos; don't create one. We grow from chaos, not because of it. Somewhere within each of us, we know this to be true. Because we all grow from chaos, some hold the hidden belief that the more chaos or crisis they find themselves in, the more growth they'll experience. These individuals we called "crisis junkies." Don't become one. Accept this time of whirlwind and upheaval; don't fight against it. If we fight it, we'll turn this chaos into a crisis for ourselves. A crisis always results from our desperate need to control the event. Understand the time(s) you're in and accept that you'll weather this storm like you have so many times before.

Lower the temperature: No, you don't need to put yourself in a freezer and lower the temperature to absolute zero (-273.15c), but you do need to lower the temperature. This is the time to pause and reflect, this is the time to process through your life's choices, and this is the time to pursue more profound and a more deeply based healing. And this is the time not to get caught up in the noise and tempest all about you. This is the time to journey within yourself. Like the boson and the fermion, lower your mental frenzy, find the silence within you, and go there. Go there, not to hide, but to process and to put your understanding and acceptance into play.

Attention: When you find yourself in the throes of chaos, don't retreat or fight it, but act; act by giving attention to where the attention is much needed; in yourself. Be gentle with yourself and respond to those inner parts of you crying out desperately to be heard. Know this to be a time for forgiveness and emotional healing, a time to pause, go inward, and attend to yourself and to visit the many of you.

You're on a great adventure. There'll be times of flowing and times of ebbing. There'll be times when you must move forward, and times when you must pause and give attention. Understand this process on your journey; accept it as a necessary condition of becoming more. Lower the temperature when times heat up and pay attention to what needs your attention. In time you'll join your fellow bosons and fermions; they who have transcended their lower forms to become the super-particles of their chosen destiny.

CHAPTER 5

The Basic Components of Reality Creation

Attend to and elevate your raw materials,
hone and sharpen the tools you work with,
develop and enhance your skills in crafting
and everything in your reality radiates.

Crafting one's reality, like crafting anything, requires materials from which to build, tools necessary for the honing and sculpting, and skills needed for a smooth and elegant completion. No person has more or fewer materials from which to work, and no one has more or fewer tools to employ, yet some individuals possess skills in crafting others have yet to cultivate. Yes, we all create our separate realities. And the realities we create, we create totally and without exception. Some create realities rife with conflict, struggle, and difficulty, while others create realities rich with light, elegance, and happiness; most create realities somewhere in between. Some mold their lives with panache, artistry, and beauty; some create lives tainted with pain, emptiness, and ugliness. Most just wing it.

Knowing and processing the raw materials and tools of reality creation, along with the willingness to practice and excel in the skills of crafting, will ensure a high quality of life. Not doing so will ensure that our life becomes a hodge-podge of good days and bad days filled with uncertainty and randomness. Our life can be a child's dabble or an artistic masterpiece, or somewhere in between.

The Raw Materials: beliefs and attitudes, thoughts and feelings, choices and decisions

Everyone uses six materials from which to structure their reality. The most successful among us do not possess more; the least successful do not have less. Materials for some are shinny and vibrant; materials for others are dull and lacking.

To elevate our reality, we must process and challenge the beliefs and attitudes we hold, the thoughts and feelings we cling to and express, and the choices and decisions we make. We mold our reality out of these raw materials. To change your reality, we must know and process each. We must replace the weak ones and enhance the stronger.

All our perceptions and perspectives are conditioned by what we believe, think, and feel. If we believe we're a victim, we attract realities that will prove we're correct. If we think we're not worth loving, we'll wall ourselves off from love. If our feelings are rooted in loneliness and despair, our perceptions will place loneliness and despair everywhere we look, and our perspectives will be dark and limiting.

Our attitudes will elevate or diminish us, and the choices and decisions we make will determine the directions our lives take.

Our reality will become more or become less or exist in a perpetual state of mediocrity based on what we hold to be true, what we maintain in attitude, what we feel and think, and what choices and decisions we make.

You and only you can process and change these raw materials. You and only you can choose to change them or choose to maintain their current place in you. These are the building blocks of your existence. They can be of straw, wood, or brick; it's your call.

Of the six raw materials, the most powerful is choice. Always be particularly vigilant of the choices you're making. What you choose is what you become. You can choose to become more or choose to become less or choose to allow others, things, or circumstances to determine the direction for you. Either way, you're the one who's ultimately choosing and deciding.

The Tools: desire, imagination, expectancy.

Along with the raw materials, there are three tools from which to work. We use these tools to form, mold, and shape the raw materials of our reality. Again, no one has more, and no one possesses less. Some, however, use these tools masterfully; others less so.

The first tool in reality creation is desire. The strength or weakness of one's desires will invite the means for their manifestation, or weaken their actualization. If your desire is weak, the attraction is weak. If your desire is strong, the attraction amplifies. Monitor your desires; if what you're pursuing are your desires, and not the desires of others, your ability to achieve increases. Always process the desires you hold and ask yourself if what you're striving for belongs to you or is expected of you by parents, consensus expectations, ego fulfillment, or your child or adolescent fantasies. If your desires do not belong exclusively to you, you'll lessen your ability to manifest them or diminish the sense of fulfillment if you do manifest them.

The second and most important of the tools is imagination. We cannot desire something if we cannot imagine it. Imagination is our sixth sense. The strength and depth of our imagination are vital to our reality creation. Dreaming, imagining, and visioning are necessary for the manifestation of our future and in living a life of our preference and choice. How can we attract desires if we limit our ability to imagine them? Strengthen the imagination, deepen its realness and value to you, and you can make what was once probable, possible, and what was once possible, actual.

Consensus thinking often limits imagination by labeling it as the frivolous and the idle past-time of day-dreamers, the lazy, and according to chauvinist distortion, the silly musings of women. Do not buy into this nonsense and distorted thinking.

The third tool is expectancy. You may possess a strong desire and a fertile imagination, but if your expectancy is weak, your capacity to attract is non-existent. For many, expectancy is dropped and substituted with something else: cynicism, doubt, denial, fear, struggle, or dismissal.

"I desire the car. I can imagine the car. But I'll probably never get it." (cynicism or doubt)

"I desire the car. I can see it clearly. Now I need to bust my ass to make it happen." (struggle)

To create realities of your choice and preference, always sharpen and hone the tools used in the crafting of them.

The Skills: discipline, love, courage, self-trust, gratitude, hope.

We can possess vibrant and well-processed raw materials. We can use sharpened and honed tools. But without skill, our reality creating can be rife with struggle and effort, often limiting and lacking in richness and fulfillment. Like any creator, we must develop skills to master our craft and elevate those skills, in time, to the level of artistry. There are many skills we can harness, but the most important are discipline, love, courage, self-trust, gratitude, and hope.

Foster discipline in yourself and all your undertakings, especially those undertakings involving your growth and awakening. To master any crafting, we must be disciplined in our work and practice. Our reality creating goes best when we have focused attention, will, and a steady resolve and commitment. True mastery is never a part-time endeavor. We must prioritize our pursuit, and we must be constant and diligent in its execution. Take your reality-creating seriously and never waiver from your dreams and your futures call.

Love is an essential skill to cultivate. When you put love into your work, your work becomes play, and your activity becomes fluid and elegant. Always nurture the power of love in you and always allow its strength to carry you. Become a master at loving and an artist in its execution.

Courage is the willingness to tell yourself the truth. Be honest in your pursuits, avoid your ego's lies and distortions, and be willing and strong enough to receive. But more importantly, be courageous enough to allow the receiving. Commit to your crafting, and seeing it through to its ultimate completion. Be courageous always in the pursuit of the truth of you, and be brave enough to discover and admit your resistance to such truth. And above all, be courageous in pursuing your beauty, truth, and goodness. It's in such light pursuits that you'll need courage the most.

Self-trust is an essential skill to develop. It's perhaps the most important. Always be willing to trust yourself more and more and ever grow and honor your unique process. Trusting the path you're on and the many along the way that will champion, protect, and guide you are crucial to your success. You cannot fail in the pursuit of your destiny, but you can slow its realization down. Self-trust will lessen your resistance. Self-trust will take time and patience and forgiveness, but the time and attention spent will be well worth it.

Gratitude is a powerful generating energy, and it's so much more than merely being thankful. By cultivating gratitude, we open ourselves to generating more reasons to be grateful. Happiness and joy reside in gratitude, as well as the ever-unfolding realization that we're loved, guided, and always protected. Practice gratitude; it will take you to heights unimaginable.

Hope is a masterful skill to possess and develop. Consensus thinking often considers hope as the desperate act of desperate people, or the idle past-time of day-dreamers and wishful thinkers. Avoid such erroneous beliefs. Cultivate the fertile richness of hope in you. Along your journey, during those times of darkness and chaos, the light of hope will guide you through. Hope will lift your dreams into manifestation and will be a light upon your journey of becoming more. Hope is very much missing in the world today. Don't let it be missing in you.

Skills need practice; daily practice. If you desire to be a masterful musician, you must practice, practice, and practice again and again. If you wish to be an artist, you must steadily work on it every day. If you want to be a master at the living of your life, you must persist in processing and strengthening your raw materials. You must persist in understanding and honing your tools of manifestation. And you must practice daily the skills necessary for bringing into form, with elegance and grace, your dreams and your shining futures.

CHAPTER 6

The Basic Components of Self-Change

*All change occurs instantaneously;
it unfolds, however, over time.
The work of healing begins
when the choice to change is made.*

People often misunderstand the concept of change, and, as such, often misuse the word. For many, *'change'* is just another way of saying *'fix.'* Change, for many, is an act of improving or repairing. Upgrading and repairing something is not changing; it's fixing. For example, if I paint my house and add a new guest room, I did not change my house, I altered it, I made it different. Hopefully, I made it better. But fixing something is not changing it. Change is not making something different or producing something better; it's moving to something new. A new home replaces your present living condition.

When you take medication, you alter the symptoms of a particular sickness; but you did not change the illness itself. Only when you move beyond the condition and move beyond the need for the condition do you change, do you become healed. If I have a problem with mosquitoes, I can spray the swamp, killing the mosquito larvae. This spraying will fix the problem, although temporarily. The mosquitoes will return. Or, I can change the mosquito problem by draining the swamp, thus addressing the root cause. I've now permanently eliminated the condition.

Like fixing and changing, curing and healing are also often misunderstood and commonly used interchangeably to refer to the same thing. Although both have the objective of ending a problem, be it physical, mental, emotional, or spiritual, what it means to heal is vastly different from what it means to cure. While curing is the ending of suffering, healing goes further by ending the root cause of the condition responsible for the suffering, the draining of the swamp if you will. The differences are in space and time. Curing is temporary; healing is ever-lifting and evolving. Curing fixes us; healing changes us.

Fixing and curing both take place upon the continuum of space and time. But all change happens instantaneously, transcending and altering space and time itself. Although change occurs in an instant, we experience it playing out in our reality over time. This 'playing out' is the play of healing, and this play facilitates the changing of space and time. Healing awakens a new you by transcending the 'you' you once were. The reason why change plays out over time is due to our belief and investment in linear reality.

All human beings have a love affair with a straight line. We need to make everything into one. Concepts of past and future, and our perception of history, are a few examples of this linear thinking. Along this straight line, we create time and space to compartmentalize, navigate, and manage our linear view of reality. In truth, all things do not exist in a straight line from a beginning to an end. Existence plays out in the eternal continuum of a moment. Within that singularity of existence, within that moment, we fix or cure within the illusion of time and space and change and heal by transcending the illusion itself.

Healing is not linear; it's a spiral. Healing always spirals upward without end. Healing always gives way to more healing. Healing is eternal. Clients often feel they're going around in circles when issues re-appear over and over again. If healing is indeed taking place, this belief in their *'going around in circles'* is not correct because of the spiraling nature of the healing process. The issue undergoing healing may come back around, but it never comes back around at the same place. Healing always occurs at deeper and deeper levels and will continue to do so until the issue is transcended. Healing spirals upward at higher and higher points along the spiral, and healing always leads to more significant and grander levels of healing. Clients may complain that they keep slipping back into their old patterns of behavior, but in truth, they're not in the same place along the spiral.

For example, let's say you've quit smoking, and it's been a while since you've had a cigarette. But now and then, you sneak out to the tool shed to light up. Ok, no big deal. No, you didn't fail, and no, you're not a failure. And no, you're not backsliding. You had your quick fix, now go on with your life and continue smoke-free. And if now and then you sneak out to the tool shed, again, no big deal. The point is that even though you healed your smoking habit, the urge to smoke at some faint level will always be there. The difference is you're controlling the condition, not the condition controlling you. You've transcended the need to smoke. The occasional urge to light-up is at a higher rung on the spiral. In time, even the urge to smoke will disappear. You may let go of a stick of butter, but the grease remains. In time the grease wears off. The important thing is to let the stick of butter go. Letting the butter go is the first step to healing.

*Remember, healing always comes back around,
but never in the same place.*

Self-change is the process of becoming more, not better, not fixed, not cured, but more. Becoming more elevates one to higher expressions of one's self. It's a never-ending process of awakening more and more to one's Truer Self. Self-change is a journey, not a destination. It never ends because the more you change and heal, the more and deeper the change and healing that waits before you. Your Truer Self is not finite; it infinite. Your Truer Self is always expanding and becoming more. The eternal spiral upward has no finishing point. Although the journey is never-ending, there are plateaus along the way. There will always be plateaus. It's on the plateaus you rest and re-fit for the adventures that await you.

Self-change can be a difficult process or an elegant one; it's what you make of it. The process can also be slow and cumbersome, or it can move at a quicker pace. The following suggestions, when put into practice, will smooth out the journey and make it more rewarding and more adventurous for you. Follow these basic-components, and you'll awaken more of your authorship and more of your skill in crafting.

Attend to the Whispers and Shouts

The bubble always rises to the surface, remember? Your outer reality is only an out-picturing of your inner one. Whatever lies within you in need of attention and healing will and must surface in your life in the form of events, circumstances, and what people often call "fate."

What needs attention and healing always surfaces first as a whisper, but when left unaddressed, it will, in time, become a shout.

For example, if you know someone who has recently been diagnosed with cancer, this may be a whisper to you to pay attention to your hidden rage, since cancer is often a metaphor for rage. If, however, you're the one diagnosed with cancer, it's a shout to address the issue, and to do so urgently.

Healing and changing means healing and changing at the source; you. Learn to pay attention to your unconscious and subconscious attempts to communicate with you and always respond to their messages. They're there to help you, not to punish you. They're essential allies on your journey; approach them as such.

Live your life consciously, pay attention to your reality, and always respond to its many calls; these are the fundamental components to self-change.

Process and Program

Never take your life for granted. Pay attention to the W's and the H: the why, when, where, who, and how of your current actions, beliefs, choices, decisions, thoughts, and feelings. Process your raw materials, process and hone your tools of manifestation, and process the strengths and weaknesses in your skills in crafting. Doing so is the work of the seeker; this is the activity of the C.O.R.E. process. For example,

Why am I allowing this into my reality?
When do I allow love in; when do I push it out?
Where are my fears clustered?
Who am I giving my reality to?
How do I respond when love and fear become too real?

Growth is hard work, but it doesn't have to be difficult work. Growth is not for the lazy or for those who feel entitled. You must pursue your objectives with due diligence and attention, and response. You must break yourself down before you can build yourself up.

Life ebbs and flows. There will be times when you must ebb and slow down to process, to program, to nurture, and to re-assess. And there will be times when you must flow and put into play all you've processed and programmed.

Process out the old; program in the new.

Once you've processed the stuff of your current patterns of behavior, your obstacles and resistances, your current limiting self-image, the lies you tell yourself, etc. you're ready to program in the new energies of what you're now becoming. Whatever you release from within you, you leave a space in need of filling. Choosing and programming new behaviors, processed and precise raw materials, new dreams and visions, and a new self-image fills that space within you.

Processing and programming is the 'H' word: home-work. You may not want to do it, but your growth requires you do so.

Use Technique

Changing and healing will accelerate through the use of technique(s) to set the changing and healing in motion. Technique(s) is an important ritual to re-programming the subconscious and responding to the calls and whispers of the unconscious. Of the many techniques available, meditation is the most powerful and effective. Meditation accomplishes three things; attract something into your life, remove something from your life, and bring to conscious awareness your resistance to allowing the first two to happen.

There are two kinds of meditation: active and passive. Active meditation programs and opens communication directly between the conscious, subconscious, and unconscious minds through the use of the powerful tool of imagination. Passive meditation quiets the mind to a profound state of physical stillness and deep mental silence to experience maximum brain coherence. Active meditation communicates; passive meditation transcends mental activity. For the working of C.O.R.E., active meditation is strongly recommended.

The language of the Unconscious is myth, metaphor, archetype, and symbol. Imagination speaks this language.

For example, if one wants to access unconscious metaphor or symbology, one would not say meditatively, *"I'd like to connect with the Unconscious."* The Unconscious does not speak English. One would meditatively imagine oneself entering and descending a dark cave or a dark opening in the ground. The image of a 'dark cave' and a 'dark opening in the ground' is a metaphor the Unconscious understands. Instead of saying meditatively, *"I'd like to address my issues with rage,"* one would journey to the lair of one's Rage Beast and face its wrath and hurt.

Meditation is not merely the act of mental story-telling. Each image and each event must be carefully selected to convey the appropriate symbol, metaphor, archetypal image, and myth. Otherwise, we're wasting our time.

Imagination is a powerful tool to use in our changing and healing work; use it and use it often. It's the most natural and most effective passageway between you and your hidden inner world, the starting point of all your reality.

Refer to Appendix Two: Techniques for some of the meditations used in C.O.R.E. work.

Be Willing and Allowing

It's one thing to choose to change; it's another to receive the change. Many are not willing to receive, and of those who are, many will not allow the receiving. Why?

Process your issues with receiving. Why are you reluctant to allow the change to occur? Why are you afraid of being successful? All success has, at its basis, the receiving of love. When you manifest any success in your life, it's because you allowed, at some level, love into your life. Therefore, reluctance to be willing or allowing of the change, the success, speaks of issues around receiving love. Ask yourself;

Am I reluctant to give up control?

Do I feel undeserving of love?

Does my arrogance dictate that
"I and only I will make it happen?"
"I don't require other's help or other's love!"

Is my issue with entitlement my need to be given, without having to take responsibility for crafting my own reality?

Is my fear of change, and the fear of the unknown that always accompanies change, preventing my receiving?

Process all that stands in your way of being willing to change, and your reluctance to allowing it to happen. When you process out the old beliefs and limitations, and then program in the new, you can move forward changed, healed, and loved.

CHAPTER 7

Beyond Curing, Beyond Fixing

Beyond the triumph of curing, healing waits.
Beyond the satisfaction of fixing, change calls.
Celebrate the curing and the fixing,
then reach for the splendid magnificence of healing
and changing sourced in you.

The goal of medicine is to end a client's suffering, and the work of health practitioners is in restoring a client to a state of wellness and vibrancy, both beautiful and noble pursuits. But the focus of ASAT™ C.O.R.E Counseling is different. Its objective is in helping those who seek becoming more through the pursuit of elegance and magic, and the awakening of conscious awareness and authorship. The ultimate of ASAT™ C.O.R.E.

Counseling is in helping one live a life beyond suffering and even living a life beyond wellness and vibrancy. Its grace is in awakening one to a reality lived in wholeness, freedom, magical synchronicities, and joy.

We're all on a magnificent journey, a journey of becoming more. Some paths traveled are more elegant than most, some less so. How people choose to travel on their journey of becoming more is not intended as an indictment or an endorsement, just a statement that the choices we make, elevating or limiting, produce the quality and quantity of the life lived. The choices we make will result in a stress-filled and difficult life, or a life more fun and adventurous. Choices can be changed, and as such, the nature of the journey we travel. Our lives were never intended to be as difficult as we're making it. We all have the power to make better choices and live happier lives.

The ASAT™ C.O.R.E. map to living serves best those willing to exercise responsibility, not guilt, for how their lives unfold. It serves best those who choose to travel adventurously, pursuing challenges more than conflict, elegance more than struggle, and the uplifting rewards of efforting more than the debilitating pain of effort and hardship. And it serves best those who wish to heal more than cure and to change more than fix, and especially those who want to journey beyond such things as healing and changing.

The ASAT™ C.O.R.E. map serves those who choose to awaken to the truth of 'who' and 'what' they are. It does not help those who wish to remain imprisoned in a story unreflective of their worth and value.

And the ASAT C.O.R.E. map serves those in search of a magical, exceptional life, not a life of mediocrity, lacking in true fulfillment and bounty.

Understanding the nature of reality creating is needed on our journey, and being accepting of life's many challenges and opportunities imperative. One must cultivate the power of forgiveness: the forgiveness of one's self, and the forgiveness of others. And one must possess the patience required to carry this forgiveness through to its completion. And being diligent in the working of the mechanics of our reality creation is vital for the journey's ultimate success.

Yes, we all create our reality. And, yes, there are no exceptions to this. And, yes, we can know and strengthen our materials out of which we're building this reality and hone and sharpen the tools we're using to mold it. And, yes, we can practice the skills used in our crafting. But understanding how our reality comes into being and how it grows and becomes stronger is valuable to keep in our awareness. Knowing this will help us change; it will help us in processing our materials, tools, and developing our skills.

How do thoughts and beliefs grow and become more powerful? This process we must explore. For there are thoughts we have, and beliefs and ideas we hold, that will impede and resist our journey of becoming more. Some of these thoughts and beliefs, if allowed to get stronger, and are left unattended, will ultimately destroy us.

Let's begin by understanding the very nature of evolution itself. Evolution has a set of laws that apply to everything in existence, from formless resonance (i.e., thoughts and ideas) to physical form.

The Laws of Evolution: The Growth of Thoughts and Ideas

1. Once something has formed, it needs to maintain and reproduce itself in the same form.

2. To accomplish this, the form needs external energy (i.e., food, energy, attention.)

3. Thoughts and ideas are forms. To survive, they must have external energy (food). The food they use is attention.

4. A form will compete with other forms for energy.

5. The form that gets the most attention (food) is the form that grows the strongest and lives the longest. Taking attention back does not mean ignoring it, but instead recognizing it, acknowledging it, releasing it, and then placing your attention elsewhere.

6. When a form gets too efficient in its consumption of energy, there's a risk that it will consume the source of that energy. The consumption of energy from its source can either result in destruction or evolution.

7. Evolution can take two directions: harmony or entropy. Assuring harmony involves (1) Choice (2) Spirituality (3) Creation of new forms (futures) toward which evolution can move toward complexity.

Humans are an excellent example of how the Laws of Evolution work. Humans are the most evolved forms on our planet; we've won the evolution challenge. We've surpassed all other species and forms through our intelligence and authority. But without responsibility and determined and robust stewardship of our world, our source of external energy, we run the risk of consuming the very planet that provides us life.

Thoughts and ideas, being non-physical forms (resonance), exist and grow in the same way. For example, if a child holds the belief that he or she is flawed, defected or broken (shame), that belief, that resonance, is now birthed and in need of external energy to grow and survive. If the child, in its growing and maturing, sustains this shame by the energy he or she feeds it, by the attention he or she provides, that shame grows more independent and becomes more powerful. Now in his or her adult years, shame has become so strong it runs the risk of consuming the source of its fuel, the one who birthed it.

We must process through our raw materials of thoughts and feelings, choices and decisions, and beliefs and attitudes to stop the feeding of these destructive forms. If we don't do this, our reality will reflect our self-consuming through illness, crisis, or other means that trigger pain and suffering and, ultimately, death. We must release all the harmful and destructive forms we've given life and power by the attention we've provided.

Ending Destructive Thoughts and Ideas

Now is the time for action. And now is the time to take back the attention we feed our harmful and destructive thoughts and beliefs and resonances. We do this by processing what we give our attention to, exposing the hidden intentions underneath them, by monitoring the actions we take, and re-scripting our old limited self-image.

Attention: Attention is your energy, etheric, and psychic, which gathers the information that is your illusion (reality). It lifts the illusion out of the subconscious and unconscious and gives it form in your reality. It allows that form to exist and to continue to exist. What you pay attention to will take structure in your reality.

Intention: Intention is what links together, gives meaning to, and prioritizes the information you gather.

Action: Action is the expression and reflection of your attention and intention. Every action, at its basis, has as its underlying intention to show you who, or what, you think you are. Actions are always a reflection of your self-image.

Self-Image: Image is what you imagine yourself to be, and what you imagine yourself to be is what you're becoming. What you're becoming is creating who you are today.

It's not necessary to change all four, but it wouldn't hurt to process them. Like four legs on a table, pull one, and the others follow. Change what you give attention to, and your intentions, actions, and self-image become different. Change your intentions and what you give attention to changes, as well as your actions and self-image.

To discover and change your self-image, do the written exercise found in Appendix Two: Techniques.

It's not necessary to process and program such changes if all you want is to cure and fix. But if you wish to live a life beyond curing, and if you desire to become more rather than settle for fixed, the work ahead of you will be well worth your time and energy.

We've explored in Part 1 the science and fundamentals of reality creation and reality changing. It was necessary to do so to establish a foundation for the work ahead. It will prove valuable to a better understanding of the nature of the C.O.R.E. map we cover in Part 2.

Each of us is on a journey of becoming more. We can undertake our journey consciously or unconsciously. I recommend consciously. We can travel our destined path, laughing and singing or crying and weeping. I recommend laughing and singing. We can take the way of masterful craftsmanship or remain hidden in the false security of a mediocre life of struggle, hit or miss uncertainty, and always at the whims of fate. It's your call. It's your choice.

> *It's not in the past you'll find your healing*
> *but upon the road ahead of you.*
> *Keep facing the future you place before you.*
> *And when the past arises to block your way,*
> *then take it as it comes.*

PART 2

Following the C.O.R.E. Map Home

CHAPTER 8

So, What's Up?

*Whatever surfaces in life is either in need of healing
or a reflection of healing accomplished.
Whatever surfaces in life is either in need of attention
or in need of acknowledgment and celebration.*

I begin each session by asking my client, *"So, what's up?"* I do this not because I wish to come off as hip and cool, which I assure you I'm not, but out of a desire to know what's surfacing in his or her life at present.

All the issues we face and deal with in life, and all those issues requiring help in their healing and resolving, emerge from the same source. And all the crises and obstacles we face in life, whether health-related, emotion-related, relationship related, or anything else related, come from the hidden depths of one's unconscious. Like the bubble in the pond, what requires attention will always float to the surface; it must, for that's the only way we'll be able to address and heal it. In its surfacing, there'll be whispers, faint at first, but growing louder and louder the closer it reaches the top; when it comes to the surface, then we'll experience its shout; then the need for response becomes urgent.

Unlike most healing systems, C.O.R.E. does not wait for the issue, or bubble, to reach the surface; it addresses the potential problem as it surfaces; it pays attention to its many whispers. But, most importantly, our clients, by paying attention and following the C.O.R.E map, learn to process their emerging issues by strengthening the raw materials in need of strengthening, by honing the tools in need of sharpening, and by mastering the skills required for a more elegant self-healing. By combining the processing skills with the powerful techniques they've learned, they become exceptional self-healers. The ultimate measure of our success is in the clients' willingness and courage to undertake, on their own, the work required for their individual growth and change.

We work in partnership with the Unconscious, Sub-Conscious, and Conscious minds to identify and interpret the information they provide, information necessary for healing. All three aid in our change and growth. It's what they're designed to do.

Remember, the need for healing is not a result of a failure, but a call to become more; it's an opportunity the C.O.R.E. map will seize upon and pursue. Nothing in life can harm us unless we allow it so. Everything in our reality directs us to the more of us if we'll only take the time to look and respond to *"what's up"* in us.

The Three Minds

Unconscious Mind: The Unconscious holds everything before and after it becomes observed. Reality is just the illusion of what exists in the more real of the Unconscious. The Unconscious has no boundaries or limits; it's also ever-expanding. The Unconscious holds the pre-conceptual and pre-structural, and thus contains all form and information before it becomes form and before it becomes actualized in 'formation.' As such, you cannot experience its magnitude or avail yourself of its range and power unless you, yourself, are unconscious; but in a state of deep sleep, you exist without form within the vastness of the Unconscious. You don't remember being there because, of course, you were unconscious.

Subconscious Mind: The Sub-conscious holds all the templates, rules, filters, and programs you've stored there over your lifetime. What you store in the Sub-conscious will filter out everything that does not comply with those templates, rules, filters, and programs. Your Sub-conscious will never over-ride these filters. It always obeys what you program and store within it. For example, if, as an adolescent, you decided, as a result of some heartbreak and despair, that you'd never allow yourself to love deeply again, and now, as an adult, you wish to do so, the filter you've placed in the Sub-conscious will not allow such love to be experienced by you. You put the filter there as an adolescent; if you want to love more deeply, it's up to you to find it and remove it.

Always be careful what you think and say, for what you think and say may be stored within the Subconscious to become another filter.

Conscious Mind: What you experience in your reality is the product of unconscious projection. The Conscious mind downloads pre-conceptual and pre-structural information and gives it form and structure and meaning in your reality through the attention and intention you give it. The Conscious mind, like a movie projector, projects a story on a blank screen. The story, before it's becomes recorded on film, is sourced in the mind of its author. What you see on the screen is an illusion; the real is in the mind of its creator.

The Unconscious, followed by the Sub-conscious, are the two most powerful minds; the least powerful is the Conscious Mind. But the Conscious mind has an ability the others do not possess; it can make choices.

The Conscious mind gathers all the information provided by the Unconscious and Subconscious and gives it focus and direction through the power of choice. If one's choice is weak and negative, the reality created will be weak and negative. If the choice is strong and positive, the reality created will reflect its strength and positivity. Therefore, it cannot be emphasized enough how powerful the element of choice is in crafting the life we live. By consciously directing the choices we make in the direction of our becoming, and correcting the choices we've made in the past that limits our becoming, we can gather all the infinite power of the Unconscious and Subconscious and harvest an incredible future.

The Law of Action and Reaction

For every action, there is an equal and opposite reaction

A reaction in the form of resistance will always follow whatever love, growth, and success we allow into our life; the more significant the love, growth, and success, the more significant the reaction. Healing requires we understand this. Smooth passage along our unique journey requires we respond when these reactions, these resistances, occur.

Traditional counseling usually involves working to heal unresolved issues from the past; ASAT™ C.O.R.E. Counseling works to heal old patterns of behavior and other resistances to our growing and becoming; the former focuses on the past, the latter on the future. It's all a matter of perception and perspective. The C.O.R.E. map is more about our becoming and less about where we've been.

If it walks like a duck and quacks like a duck,
It's not necessarily a duck.

Your client may sound and act and bring to the session the same old 'same olds,' but the nature and trigger of the problem are vastly different. Now, every issue, every crisis, every 'same old' that comes our way is a reaction to the client's growth and becoming; every problem is a marker of change on the way to an awakening and blossoming future. This perspective is essential to maintain as it keeps our focus on the client's positive momentum rather than the rehashing of the client's perceived past mistakes and past issues. Here lies the difference between the work we do with C.O.R.E. and the work done by others.

Our clients are awakening and becoming more; as you, the counselor, are awakening and becoming more. That's why the two of you are together; that's why both your Higher Selves joined you. You're both fellow journeymen on a magnificent adventure. One is there to provide counsel and inspiration, the other to learn and grow from the help and inspiration provided. One is not better than the other, but one has journeyed the path before and knows the pitfalls, warning signs, and traps along the way. One is an experienced traveler, the other yet learning the art of traveling this new and often frightening way. But both give to the other a gift: one, the gift of healing, the other the gift of healing accepted. Both are brothers and sisters on this Grand Adventure of becoming more; both are Coming Home.

The more you become,
the greater will be your resistance.
But the more you become,
the more able you'll be to handle
and grow from it.

CHAPTER 9

The C.O.R.E Map to Self-Healing

Be a Path-Maker. Make a new path.
And in so doing, you'll awaken and inspire in others
the pursuit of their own path home.

I've often been asked to explain ASAT™ C.O.R.E. in simple terms. I found doing so to be difficult, for C.O.R.E. is continuously changing and evolving and redefining itself. Since every living thing grows and evolves, I guess C.O.R.E is a living system. Any idea or system of thought that does not grow and change is either dying or already dead. But if I were pushed, I'd describe C.O.R.E. as follows;

C.O.R.E. is an acronym for Conscious, Ownership, Release, and Engage. It's a life map that helps clients in their growing and becoming by helping in their desire to claim ownership of their unlimited capacity for conscious creation of life. C.O.R.E. helps identify and release old beliefs and hidden agendas, along with their destructive life patterns, that form the basis of all problems mental, physical, emotional, and spiritual.

The efficacy of the C.O.R.E. process shows itself in the lives of those who follow its map; lives lived bountifully, elegantly, successful, and deliberately. Its achievements express in magical synchronicities, a growing acceptance of being loved and loving, and in the awakening and claiming of one's beauty, truth, and goodness.

C.O.R.E. is not a technique, and it's not a system of healing. It's not a philosophy, a religion, nor any type of alternative New Age thinking or metaphysical mumbo-jumbo, as some like to call it. It's not a healing modality, and it's not an offshoot of any mainstream or non-mainstream healing tradition. C.O.R.E. is not new-age psychology, alternative medicine, or other healing approaches. C.O.R.E. is markedly different. And because C.O.R.E. and ASAT™ C.O.R.E. Counseling are so very different and serve clients with particular needs and priorities, they never compete with the valuable and essential services others provide.

So what is C.O.R.E.?

C.O.R.E. is a map. Like any map, it helps a traveler reach his or her destination. We can reach our desired goal by winging it, but doing so would prove time-consuming, difficult, exhausting, stressful, and potentially hazardous. Winging it will lead us down many dead ends and across many bumpy and unpaved highways. With a well-made map, one's journey will be more elegant, less fearful, and more enjoyable. A well-designed map illuminates the route and provides markers and sign-posts to assure the traveler that he or she is journeying in the right direction.

The C.O.R.E. map is more a matter of perspective and experience than adherence to some tried and proven set of rules and formulas. C.O.R.E. stands alone in the work it does; it is its own distinct profession.

All life is a journey; all life is a journey Home. C.O.R.E. will guide us upon that journey and will help us navigate its many hazards, shifting terrains, and obstacles. It will provide a clear route, voiding wasteful short-cuts that lead us nowhere, and places that will stall and hinder our advancement. The map will advise us when to rest and when to travel, and where rest-stops await us for a much-needed pause and refueling. The C.O.R.E. map is not, by far, the only route to where you're going, but it's a magical and elegant one.

C.O.R.E.'s work is not for everyone. You'll need to be called to pursue it. You'll need to be willing to respond to the challenges of the journey with courage and commitment. You'll need a willingness to tell yourself the truth, and a willingness to hear it. You'll need a willingness to lean on the grander you and to lean on the love and guidance of your Higher Self. Those who journey the C.O.R.E. map will be required to take responsibility for the path they're on and the path they've previously traveled. They should never expect their guides and counselors to assume responsibility for them. Your guides and counselors are responsible only for the map and for keeping you focused on it. You must travel on your own, and you must challenge yourself and allow yourself to be challenged along the way, and learn and reach beyond the false safely of past and familiar routes.

Though you travel on your own, you're never alone on your travels or any journey you're on. Be willing and allow that awareness to comfort and strengthen your commitment.

When you travel the road, the C.O.R.E. map suggests, know that it's you who accomplish your healing and growing, not the map, nor the one who guides and challenges you. All healing, in truth, is self-healing. But not all healing is conscious self-healing.

No, the C.O.R.E. map is not for everyone. But if you're called to it, perhaps it's a road to travel and a map for you to follow. It's your choice. It's your call.

So what is ASAT™ C.O.R.E. Counseling?

ASAT™ C.O.R.E. Counseling is a unique profession with a unique clientele. Its clients strive for higher growth, with a life of magical synchronicities. They seek a fun-filled life rich and resplendent with bountiful successes and overflowing with conscious creations. They pursue the claiming of their authorship and to use their authorship wisely and elegantly. They choose to move beyond struggle and conflict. And they choose to participate, with love and guidance, on a Grand Adventure of Coming Home

ASAT™ C.O.R.E. Counseling focuses more on where a client's going than where a client's been. It addresses all that rises to resist that going and responds to unconscious whispers and shouts in ways most others do not do. ASAT™ C.O.R.E.

Counseling's attention is on awakening a sense of wholeness and on reclaiming a life of Oneness forgotten, but not lost, a long, long time ago. ASAT™ C.O.R.E. Counseling is about Coming Home, not merely about living a better life.

> ***You are loved, and you are loving.***
> ***You are awakening and becoming.***
> ***You have so much help along the way;***
> ***just ask.***

CHAPTER 10

(C)onscious

*All healing and growing requires our being awake
and responsive.
Living consciously is the first step in C.O.R.E.
It sets all the other steps in motion.*

All healing begins with recognizing the need for healing; it involves being conscious and aware. We don't always need to know the details of what's calling for our attention, but we must be alert to its calls and whispers, and most notably, its urgent shouts.

Curing, unlike healing, does not require our being conscious and aware. We can cure without recognizing or acknowledging that which seeks our attention. If we get the proper medical attention or the appropriate treatment, we can hopefully cure and move on. We can break a leg and have it set, and in time we'll be as good as new. We don't have to respond to the messages the broken leg is sending. We can continue skating through life oblivious to our power and authority to change it. We can get by-pass surgery or the kidney removed, the prescription filled, and get on with the living of our life. We don't have to respond to the whispers of our heart or kidney, or our mental or emotional condition; we can return to our sleep, whistle past the graveyard, and continue living a blind and deaf existence.

Most people are choosing to exist and nothing more. They're choosing to live their lives unconsciously, casting their fate to the whims of luck, chance, or to the good or bad graces of a roll of the dice. They write off what happens to them as God's Will, or an act of karmic retribution or a *"Life's a bitch, and then you die"* cynical belief or being merely the victim and recipient of life's many uncertainties, quirks, and injustices.

Some take steps to hedge against the inevitable doom and gloom by getting the proper exercise, the annual medical checkups, by reading the self-help books written by smiley-faced authors, and by diligently attending church, temple, or mosque on a somewhat regular basis. Some will go so far as to obediently say their prayers at night in the attempt to appease their gods and by tithing their annual ten percent. Don't get me wrong; I'm not at all suggesting that such activities are improper or lack value, but what I am suggesting is that without conscious living and a personal sense of one's authorship, life will always be left to the whims of fate.

Such lives are not for those who pursue conscious healing. Such lives do not meet the conditions of an authored reality and are not the stuff of a responsive, deliberate life. They're not the path, the way, the journey that the C.O.R.E. map guides. C.O.R.E. is for those who wish to go beyond, not those settling for a 'get-by,' 'move on' existence.

Wanting more out of life, expecting more out of life, requires one to make conscious choices and decisions, choices and decisions based on the exercise of responsible authorship.

Yes, you can cure without being conscious; but healing, evolving, growing, and especially becoming more, demand we are. The first step, and the one that sets all the others in motion, is the willingness and the determination to pursue more conscious awareness in the living of our life.

Using their developed awareness and their deep connection to Nature, Native peoples learned to read the language of the world about them, and thus grew in their sense of Oneness with all they experienced. The Aboriginal people of Australia call the conscious state of awareness "The Dream Time," and their dreams and imagination, reality. Oh, how wonderfully aware they are!

This connection, this awareness, is much needed in the world today. We've become disconnected from our source, our Mother, and therefore disconnected from ourselves. We walk the earth alienated and apart. And we walk the earth with a deep sense of loneliness.

Cultivate the art of observation; cultivate the skill of listening and paying attention. Read the signs that are all around you; then you're taking the first step of your growing, becoming, and ultimate healing.

The language of the Unconscious is not English, French, Latin, or Swahili. The language of the Unconscious is myth, metaphor, archetype, and symbol. When the Unconscious wants your attention, it will do so, not by saying, *"Hey, Bud, have a minute? Got something I want to tell you,"* but by speaking to you in its language.

For example, if you hold deep unresolved issues around being loved and loving, the Unconscious may speak to you through issues around your physical heart (a symbol). If you hold deep within you intense anger and rage that has grown so powerful that it needs immediate attention, the Unconscious may shout out to you in the form of cancer (a metaphor). If you wallow deep in martyrhood and find yourself always struggling, pushing, and working hard and getting nowhere, the Unconscious is speaking to you in myth; in this case, the myth of Sisyphus. And if you find yourself always in need of rescuing, like some damsel in distress, the Unconscious is conveying an archetypal message.

The Unconscious is always attempting to get your attention; it's always trying to help you. By cultivating the art of listening and paying attention, as Native peoples do, you'll be able to address what needs addressing, and respond when a response is required. You'll open to a different way of living, you'll reclaim your lost, or stolen, or relinquished power, and once again become the author of your reality.

The C.O.R.E. map will help you with this if you're willing and allowing. And if you pay attention to what's up for you, and be aware and conscious of its presence, you'll heal, and grow, and thrive in ways you've yet to imagine. You'll live your life deliberately, consciously, and if you choose, and if you exercise your authorship, elegantly.

CHAPTER 11

(O)wnership

Respond when called;
then own and attend to what needs attending.
This is the process of self-healing;
this is the second step in C.O.R.E.
It connects the first with the third
and propels the healing forward.

The second step in the C.O.R.E. map is ownership. Ownership is the fulcrum between the first and the third. Without it, the C.O.R.E. map cannot work. It's one thing to be conscious and aware of the emerging issue needing attention and response; it's another to acknowledge and release it, the second and third steps. Without ownership, acknowledgment, and responsibility, releasing will not occur. We can admit to a problem, but unless we own it, make it ours, we'll not let it go because we still have an investment in it; we're still using it, we're still getting a payoff from it.

Payoffs

Payoffs are the benefits we receive from a harmful condition we engage in. For example, if I'm using martyrhood to get attention and, or to control others, the benefit is the power I feel from the attention and control. I can admit to having a martyrhood problem, I can even acknowledge that it's hurting me and others, but if I refuse to relinquish the payoff, the sense of power I receive, I'll not be willing to allow its release. In psychology, these payoffs are referred to as "secondary benefit." The term "secondary benefit" is a misnomer. It's not secondary; it's primary. I may be asking to heal my martyrhood, but my primary desire is to continue receiving its payoff. The payoff is the benefit I choose; treating my martyr is secondary to it.

We never do what we don't want to do, and we always do what we want. The key is in knowing the truth of what we want and don't want. The C.O.R.E. map requires the exposure of these hidden payoffs, these 'wants' and 'don't wants,' before we choose to own it. It requires being conscious at a deeper level, and then to move forward by asking the question, *"What is it I really want, here?"* If I'm asking for the healing but holding out for the payoff, I'm just paying lip service to the C.O.R.E. Map. I don't desire, and therefore won't allow, Step 3, release.

With very few exceptions, no one wants to suffer; no one wants cancer, the heart condition, the broken leg, and no one wants to die. No one wants the pain, the hurt, the loneliness, the fear, etc., that the harmful conditions trigger. But what people desire most may be just what the contributing conditions provide. Unless the true desires are made conscious, and until a willed choice is made to admit to it and own it, deciding to let it go will not occur. One may hate the pain and suffering their drug use causes, but if they want to lose themselves in the high more, they'll not heal the problem.

Ownership of what we've consciously acknowledged propels us to the next step in the process, release; it places us in the position of having to choose to continue forward with the map or not. Some clients will not go to the next level. This is ok. At least the client went this far. In time, they may make a different choice. The counselor must never push nor nudge, nor in any way, encourage that different choice. Choice is a gift from God/Goddess/All That Is; it's not our place to interfere with it. The role of the counselor is to place the cards on the table and let the client choose.

Ownership means taking responsibility without going into guilt or self-blame. Guilt and self-blame diminish our resonance and negates the power of our ownership. Taking responsibility for our life is the first step in reclaiming authorship. Without the willingness to author our reality, and without re-claiming that authorship, we'll give our authorship over to others, events, fate, or circumstances. Above all, we must avoid this. Without authorship, we can cure, but not heal, fix, but not change. Without ownership, responsibility, and authorship, we only change cosmetically; real change, real growth, eludes us.

The 'R' Word

Responsibility: the quality or state of being accountable. (Merriam Webster's Dictionary)

The word 'responsibility,' like the word 'homework,' does not elicit strong positive responses due to past experiences and the term's negative implications. It's not something we want to do. Although I did have a student who told me she loved and looked forward to doing homework. That's just weird!

Responsibility for some is the 'R' word, the unappetizing call to a duty or an obligation we must perform, whether we want to or not. It's also a term used to lay blame or quilt, not something about which to get all warm and fuzzy over.

"It's time to come in and do your homework, Johnny!"

"Now Mary, remember, you're responsible for your little brother. Take him with you and your friends to the mall."

"I didn't do it, Billy did! He's responsible!"

"That *#%* president is responsible for all my *#%* unhappiness!"

"It's not you, Bob, it's just me. I'm responsible."
(meaning Bob's responsible)

And on, and on, and on it goes.

Responsibility has come to mean anything but taking action to address a wrong or, like any responsible adult, to be accountable for one's life; it's more accurate meaning. Just say the word and do nothing, that's enough; the *"buck stops here"* and goes no further. When a celebrity or politician stands before the lights and cameras and declares, *"I take full responsibility for my actions!"* rest assured the problem will stop there and go no further. Nothing will get resolved, and nothing will take place to correct it. On April 19, 1993, Attorney General Janet Reno declared, *"I take full responsibility,"* for the massacre in Waco, Texas, that saw 80 people, mostly children, senselessly killed by federal agents under her watch. Since then, nothing was ever put into place to prevent it from happening again. Responsibility stopped with the simple declaration, *"I take full responsibility."*

However, responsibility, in its true meaning, is to 'respond to a call for action.' We hear the call, we respond, and thus take responsibility, not guilt. Respond is what adults do when the needs and obligations of life call one to action, to healing. In responding, we consciously initiate growth and change; this is ownership, the second step in the C.O.R.E. map. When the Unconscious calls us to action, we respond. When any part of our self cries out, we respond, we own, we act.

Taking responsibility, accepting ownership, is a condition necessary for any healing to occur. Yes, you can cure a health problem without taking responsibility, but you'll never heal the issue until you do. Without healing, the problem will, and must, surface again in a similar or not so similar form.

Responsibility means 'to respond.' It means taking action, address what needs addressing, and initiate the change necessary to end it. Responsibility and ownership are powerful magical forces that open one to unlimited opportunities for unparalleled healing and growth.

As stated earlier, whatever we've shoved in our unconscious, good or bad, in this lifetime or another, will in time surface and become conscious to us. All health issues, life issues, emotional issues, etc. are sourced in the Unconscious. But these issues do not become conscious without warning. When they initially surface, they appear as whispers, and when not responded to by taking responsibility and ownership, they will, in time, appear as shouts. Respond to the whispers, and you'll no longer have to contend with the shouts, which can, over time, prove deadly.

The purpose of life is to learn to enjoy it and to create it consciously. And the goal is to awaken more and more of one's Truer Self. Anything less is a distraction and a waste of a perfectly good lifetime. Responsibility is a gift we give ourselves that, when used, will allow us to become more of who we are and to enable us to live our life's purpose with success and fun. To awaken the magic of responsibility, work with the techniques found in Appendix Two.

Cause and effect are not how things or events become a reality; resonance is. Whenever we get caught in the cycle of cause and effect, we are, in truth, engaging in resonance causation. It feels like we're out of control because we've given power over to it. For example, a careless driver hits your car. Your natural reaction is to blame the other driver and the event for your discomfort. It's true, the driver hit your car and initiated the situation, and it's ok to get angry and upset at him; to do otherwise would put yourself in denial. The real source of the discomfort is not in the other driver or the accident; they're just the 'button-pushers.' The real source of the anger and pain is within you. Get angry, be upset, but step back when you're in a place that's conducive to do so and check-in with yourself. You'll find a tremendous opportunity for deep healing if you're willing to exercise responsibility and willingness to own the event at its source; you.

The accident is a shout from your unconscious that something requires urgent attention. It took the accident to bring it to you. Step back from what you think is the cause, the accident, and address what needs addressing; the real issue existing within you. Listen and attend to the shouts of your anger, fear, pain, etc. It's sourced in a place very deep in you, not from the accident. Your outer reality always reflects your inner one. Don't give away your power to a false story; instead, use your power to respond to the real issue in need of healing and choose to lift it with elegance and dignity. Own your life, and from that place of ownership, change it.

The more responsibility you assume in the living of your life, the greater will be the awakening of your authorship of it.

CHAPTER 12

(R)elease

*Releasing and letting go takes the
greatest amount of courage
because letting go is the hardest thing to do.
Not because the act itself is difficult, it's not,
but because of our stubborn need to keep holding on.
This is the third and most powerful step in C.O.R.E.
It will involve your will and unwavering determination.*

Releasing and letting go is essential for any healing and change to occur. Without it, there's no healing and change. Release is the third of the C.O.R.E steps; it's also the most powerful and most challenging. It needs to be powerful precisely because it's so challenging to execute. If the previous two steps are not solidly in place, being fully conscious and owning of the issue or condition, If they're weak and faulty in the slightest way, the power necessary to effect the release may not be enough to see it through.

The issue or condition requiring the healing and change has been with us for a long time. We've invested much attention and much energy to maintain and grow it. We've used and benefited from its presence, and in our younger years, may have relied on it for protection and guidance. It's familiar to us. And, as strange as it may sound, deep within, well hidden, we may even consider it a friend. And this issue or condition is deemed vital to the survival of the parts of us we call the Dark Counselors, or at least they believe it is, and they'll not be easily swayed to give it up. They'll fight hard to maintain it (See Chapter 14, *The Dark Counselors*). But in the end, it's your call and your decision whether you keep it or let it go.

If you hold a tiny pea within your hand, and, with the palm faced downward, open your hand, the little pea will easily release. But if your palm is sticky, the pea may not fall out. It's what causes the stickiness that must be processed and removed before the release can happen. To put it another way, if you're learning to swim, holding tightly to the side of the pool, for some, is a natural fear condition. In time, you must choose to let your fingers loose to set yourself free to swim. You must recognize and acknowledge your fear and decide to let it go, then take action to proceed.

The process of release is easy; the will to execute it is where the challenge lies. The third step in the C.O.R.E. process, as easy as it is to do, may involve much attention and processing, and much commitment and resolve.

Releasing and letting go can happen quickly or happen over time, depending on the resistance and the work you do to handle it. You may be required to go back to Step 1 to recognize the resistance, and then Step 2, to acknowledge its presence in you. It's when you complete Step 2, you move ahead and let go of the resistance, Step 3. Now, return once again to release and let go of the issue and condition you were previously working on.

C.O.R.E. is hard work, not difficult work. It takes much will to execute and much attention to process its many resistances and needs. But in the end, all the work involved will reward you with profound healing and change.

The Power of Forgiveness

When you're ready to release and let go, forgiveness will be the most powerful tool you can employ to make the release happen. Forgiving yourself for the issue or condition without self-blame or self-judgment, and forgiving others for what they did, or you believe they did, is necessary for real release to occur and to allow the freedom that comes from it. But just saying the words, *"I forgive,"* is not enough; it requires a deep and sincerely held realness in you. You must genuinely forgive and truly forgive honestly.

Forgiving yourself is a complex matter. It involves understanding and forgiving the many parts of you that come from places of pain, limited resources and understanding, and shame and neglect (See Chapter 14: Parts Therapy). It involves forgiving those parts of you that still hold out for pay-offs and still possess hidden agendas and psychic contracts they'll be reluctant to let go. And it involves forgiving those parts of you that are locked and imprisoned in their fears and terrors. These parts of you will be resistant to your healing and changing. They'll need your love, your understanding, and your forgiveness. Forgiving yourself can be very hard to do, but unless you take the time and make the commitment to do so, Step 3, release, will not occur.

Forgiving others is also a complex matter. Never forgive what another did to you; such forgiveness is not necessary. Pardoning another's action sends a message to the offended parts of you that their hurt and pain hold little value to you. You never want to do this. No, never forgive the act, but the one who caused the act. Forgiveness of others involves understanding; it involves understanding their weakness, their hurt, their loneliness and pain, and their deep-rooted fear and anger, and their painful existence and limited sense of self, etc. Place your attention and forgiveness on the 'why' of their actions, never the actions themselves.

Forgiveness is the ultimate healer and the ultimate liberator. Without it, you'll remain locked in your lonely prison of pain and loneliness. With forgiveness, you'll be free to soar and fly to heights of freedom and self-love and understanding.

Forgiveness is the ultimate means of release. When you're no longer carrying the baggage of hidden agendas, secret pay-offs, unresolved pains and hurts from past wrongs and deeds, you'll no longer face the resistances to your letting go. Then, like the little pea, when you open your hand, it'll quickly and easily fall away. And like learning to swim, you'll free your fingers from the side of the pool and swam the gentle waters of a calm and liberating life.

Step 3, release, the most powerful of the four, now makes way for Step 4, engage, the action that anchors the others, and leads to becoming more

CHAPTER 13

(E)ngage

*Taking action grounds you and carries you onward
to more profound healing and change.
Although 'engage' is the fourth and last step in C.O.R.E.,
It's not the final step.
There's no final step in becoming more.*

Now that we've recognized the whispers and shouts with their many calls for a response, now that we have owned and acknowledged their source in us, and through forgiveness, allowed their release, it's now time to move forward healed and changed, and to engage our life differently; it's time to take action.

Engagement is the requirement of Step 4 of the C.O.R.E. map, and it's in the act of engagement that we anchor the other three. We anchor and ground when we act with confidence and certainty in our healing and our change. We anchor and ground in our faith in our process, and we anchor and ground by engaging our reality and our future as the new and more real selves we've now become. We've freed our selves of the weighty issue or condition, but we can always bend down and pick it back up. By continuing to walk on, away from the desire and pull yet lingering, we become stronger and more anchored in our newer self.

Though healed and changed, we can always return to our past patterns of behavior. We must be diligent and watchful of its lingering calls. But the more we keep engaged, and the more we move on, the easier our journey becomes, and the less audible the lingering calls. We anchor our healing and change as we move toward the future, and we ground our healing and transformation, the more we continue to pay attention, and the more we respond to the calls.

Many people successfully complete the first three steps but fail at the fourth; this is not because they haven't healed; they have. It's because they think their healing is over when in truth, it's just beginning. Healing is a lifelong process requiring constant vigilance and awareness.

Yes, you've healed, and yes, you've changed, and, yes, you'll live the results of your healing and change, with its many gifts and treasures, but you must keep pursuing the more of you and continue on the road ahead. On your journey Coming Home, don't stop at the first rest stop and decide to go no further. Don't play it safe and take your winnings and go home; play on and keep the wheel turning. And if the game gets scary and your good fortune turns the other way, you can always use the C.O.R.E. map to load the dice and keep the game in your favor.

Many stop and give up; they stop and decide the path's too rough and turn about and go back, but you're not one of them. Yes, pause at the first rest stop, in fact, pause at all of them. Rest, refit, and refuel for the journey yet before you. But when your rest is over, and it's time for you to move on, then engage the road ahead and keep your adventure going. The way gets easier the further along you go, and the winnings keep on coming, but you'll never know this if you do not engage the road before you.

There's never an end to becoming more, and never an end to C.O.R.E. processing; becoming more does not progress in a straight line, but elevates in a spiral, and engagement never reaches a conclusion but to a higher place in our growth and awakening.

Engagement begins the process anew by leading us to the need to be more consciously aware (Step 1), and from there, to a higher level of ownership (Step 2) and release (Step 3), and a higher level of engagement (Step 4). Engaging never takes us to the same place on the upward spiral, and never the same place on our journey.

Remember, all growth, healing, and becoming more, advances us upward along an endless spiral of awareness and self-discovery. Our growing and becoming never has an end, and our happiness and joy, our successes and accomplishments, and the reclaiming of our beauty, truth, and goodness will forever be more without bounds and limits. Even after we Come Home to our Oneness with God/Goddess/All That Is, our growth and becoming more continues and blossoms.

People occasionally ask, *"Did I really heal if the problem keeps reappearing?"* The answer is always the same, *"Yes, you did."* The problem will keep reappearing again and again, but never at the same location on the spiral because it's not the same problem.

> *"If it walks like a duck and quacks like a duck,*
> *it may not be a duck."*

You're healing at ever-deepening levels and will continue to do so till the time comes when you eventually transcend all need for it. Your growth and healing deepen with each turning of the C.O.R.E. cycle, and the problem needing healing connects differently with you.

The more powerful the change, the louder the response; the deeper the healing, the more intense the healing crisis. But the good news is that as you grow and heal, you become stronger and more powerful, and more able to deal with what comes your way. Although the response is more significant, your capacity to handle it gets easier, as well as your ability to craft an elegant, more supportive, and more magical life. What once was a raging storm becomes, in time, a summer drizzle. In time, it becomes a tiny droplet barely noticeable.

CHAPTER 14

Parts Therapy: Healing the Whole of You

If you can love the least of you,
you'll most certainly love the whole.
Remember always,
you're going nowhere without them.

Whenever a lowly voice from The Great Unwashed speaks of healing one's 'Inner Child,' some among the High Gods of Psychology, and even most who conduct 'Inner Child' sessions, gaze down from the heights of their Olympian office suites, and with compassionate condescension reply,

"Oh my, what a novel concept! Yes, go ahead and do your thing if you really believe such New Age mumbo-jumbo.

But of course, you realize, don't you, that there's no such thing as an Inner Child?"

But if it works for you, well my dear, you certainly have my blessing."

They then return to their study of the sacred tomes of lofty Freudian wisdom.

But, in truth, the Inner Child is real, not a fantasy, and not a creation of New Age thinking. There's not one Inner child, but many inner children, many inner adolescents, many inner young adults, and indeed many inner 'you's.' In truth, you're not an 'I,' you're a 'we.' And all your many selves of past and future exist now, at this moment, in your current reality. Time and space are illusions, remember?

All your many lifetimes, past and future, and all the lives you've lived, and are yet to live, in this your present life, exist now. They exist in their own time and space, and like you, they're growing and becoming more. All your many lives are unfolding, within their separate illusions of space and time, on a spiraling continuum and all within an eternal moment. All of 'you' exist, all of 'you' are growing, and all of 'you' need attention, love, and healing: this is the work of Parts Therapy.

Parts Therapy is, by far, the most important and the most powerful tool in the arsenal of ASAT™ C.O.R.E Counseling. But Parts Therapy loses its potency when those conducting it minimize their work by believing it a fantasy or just a technique. In time, and with steady practice, you'll honor the many parts of you and come to respect their realness; this must happen to awaken the real experience of oneness and wholeness in you. And this must happen because you're not going anywhere without all of you coming as well.

Remember the Law of Resonance? When two or more waves meet, the higher wave will lower, or the lower will lift, or they'll meet somewhere in between. Remember? Understanding this law is important to understanding how Parts Therapy works. Here's an example; when you engage with the resonance of martyr (when you're in martyr), you'll lower your resonance to that of martyr, or you'll elevate and transform the martyr, or you'll compromise with it. The result will attract resonances (realities) that reflect and enable your lowered frequency, or reflect and enable your elevated frequency, or reflect and maintain a state of compromise between you and the resonance of martyr. In other words, you'll attract a martyred life, a magical life, or a compromised life. There's only one acceptable choice here, and that's to lift your martyr; to change its resonance, not yours.

However, when you're in a relationship with your Higher Self, or your Soul and Spirit, or God/Goddess/All That Is, they'll never lower their resonance but will lift yours instead. There's no compromise. This 'lifting' is inherent in an elevated spirituality; your relationship with that which is more than you. The relationship always lifts you. You ever become more by it.

All the various selves of the 'you' you once were, in their different times and spaces, are influenced by your resonance, your frequency, this standing wave of you. You're the grand attractor at this time and in this space. And likewise, all your future selves, both dark and light, align with you according to the resonance, lowered or heightened, you're holding today. You, being a higher resonance, can elevate your lesser selves, your younger selves. Those future selves that live a higher frequency will be attracted to you by the elevated attraction you carry.

You, at this moment, are the grand attractor for all your pasts and futures. The choices and decisions, thoughts and feelings, and beliefs and attitudes you hold and make can lift your younger selves and can align you with more awakened futures, or it can lower or compromise if those raw materials are limiting and dull. It's up to you. Your future can become a nightmare, a radiant state of light and joy, or somewhere in between. It's your call. It's your choice. It's your resonance.

Choosing to work with your various selves by giving them attention and providing them with nurturing and support is a wise choice to make on your journey of growing and become more. It will prove to be a valuable step in your total healing and the lifting of your resonance.

Attending to Your Developing Selves

Your lesser selves are not your inferior selves. They're the parts of you who possess less awareness, have fewer resources, and have less understanding and maturity. The 'you' you were at age 5 or 16 are not as evolved, not as self-aware, and not as conscious as the person you are today. Likewise, the parts of you that are more, your future selves, have more self-awareness, are more conscious, possess keener insight, and are more evolved than you.

Like you, your younger selves have a broad array of possible futures, you being one of them. Like you, they'll align with those futures that resonate with the choices and decisions, thoughts and feelings, and beliefs and attitudes they hold and make in their time and space. When you attend to them, when you give them your love, healing, understanding, and patience, you become aligned. You elevate their resonance, you inspire in them new choices and decisions, more elevated thoughts and feelings, and more productive beliefs and attitudes, and you awaken more of a sense of wholeness in all of you. You raise to a state where you genuinely love the totality of yourself and the grander 'you' you're becoming.

Since you also have a broad array of possible futures, the choices and decisions, thoughts and feelings, beliefs and attitudes you hold and make in this present time and space will align with those futures dark or light that resonates with them. By questioning and elevating your choices and decisions, by monitoring your thoughts and feelings, by challenging your beliefs and attitudes, you lift your resonance to align with the more real you, those futures that resonate more with the 'you' you're destined to become.

By attending to your younger selves and by leaning on the parts of 'you' more real, the more magical, the more evolved, and the more consciously aware you'll become, and the more powerful will be the realities you, the grand attractor, will draw to you. You'll embark on a journey more magnificent than anything you can yet fathom. You'll become that grander you beyond the limits of what you currently imagine, you'll more elegantly and gracefully travel your destined journey of Coming Home, and you'll do so by way of fun, magic, and bountiful adventure rather than through the rigors and struggles of others. What was impossible once is possible today; what is possible today becomes probable tomorrow, and what is probable tomorrow will actualize in the future. All this happens through the simple act of shifting resonance.

Although your younger selves are not aware of 'you' their future, they're influenced by you. What you believe, the attitudes you have, what you feel and think, and what choices and decisions you make will affect them. It resonates with them since you all share the same moment with different frequencies. Change and hone these raw materials, and you'll lift their resonances and elevate their frequencies.

You are likewise not aware of your future selves, but like your younger selves, you too are influenced by their higher resonances and elevated frequencies. They will lift your resonance and elevate your frequency if you're in alignment with them.

You're the singular representative, in this time and space, of all the many parts of you; past and future. The resonance you hold aligns you and your past with futures dark or light. Your future comes into alignment with you, the grand attractor. And since all your thoughts and feelings, choices and decisions, and beliefs and attitudes contribute to the synergy that is your resonance, elevating these raw materials aligns you with elevated futures and lifts the resonances of your younger developing selves. You cannot change the details of your past, but you can alter the outcomes, and especially the effects they have on you today. You cannot know what your future holds, but you can be lifted by it, assuming you're aligning with futures more real and more luminous.

Being attentive and nurturing to your lesser selves, and being willing to be attended to and nurtured by the more real you, are wise choices to make. They'll ensure a more elegant journey of becoming more.

You can navigate more elegantly through life by attending to your lesser selves who reside within your unconscious. You can evolve more gracefully by choosing to respond to their whispers instead of reacting to their many cries and shouts.

Use the Parts Meditation found in Appendix Two: Techniques. Use it regularly to respond to the whispers of your less developed selves and to those we call "The Dark Counselors." And pay particular attention to the suggestions outlined in the section, *'Essential Points to Consider When Attending to Your Developing Selves and Dark Counselors.'*

Following these suggestions, and doing the Parts Meditation, will change your resonance. You'll experience magic unfolding, you'll awaken more profound healings, and you'll experience true wholeness. And you'll discover the luminous love you genuinely have for yourself.

The Dark Counselors

In addition to your younger biological selves, there are resonances you formed alliances with, energies to help you handle the many pains and terrors of childhood and adolescence. These resonances are parts of you now, and like your biological selves, must be given attention.

Everyone engages these resonances to a greater or lesser degree. It was to your credit that you made such alliances;

without them, you may not have survived the rigors of growing up. Although these resonances are harmful and destructive, they fulfilled their function in keeping you safe and able to cope. But now that you're an adult these energies, having grown more potent, will impede and destroy you over time.

The following are a few of the Dark Counselors you engage in your day to day life, and to whom you give your power. There are others, but these are the more dominant. Of these energies, your Negative Ego is the strongest and most troublesome. You will read more about them in Chapter 20: The Hidden Killers.

Negative Ego: The function of the Negative Ego is to provide information for your interpretation. But time and time again, it was expected to do the interpreting, a task it was doomed to fail. Over time it came to hate you for this, and now it seeks to destroy you. Your negative ego always lies to you.

The Dominator (Control): It came into being during your youth as a protector to keep you safe from fear. When you felt frightened and out of control, it encouraged more control and domination from you.

The Martyr: The Martyr is the silent sufferer who needs an audience to witness its melodrama of being unloved, unappreciated, or overworked. Its influence in your life pushes love away.

Rage: Rage is the highest frequency of anger. As a natural human emotion, it has opposing values: Enrage (negative) - a fit of deep and intense anger, highly charged, that gnaws at and tears down an individual over time. Outrage (positive) - an expression of anger, highly charged, that can motivate one to change.

The Terrorist: During your youth, you tasked the Terrorist with halting you from stepping too far beyond control. Its function was to blow-up your reality and to instill fear so you won't relax your guard. The terrorism we see in the world is an out-picturing of each person's inner terrorist.

The Chauvinist: The Chauvinist kept you safe by denying or minimizing the power of feminine energy. Its distorting energy, however, castrates masculine energy in men and devalues the power of feminine energy in women.

In your youth, you sought the counsel and guidance of these dark ones, especially that of your Negative Ego. It was not because you were wrong or bad; you simply had very few choices at the time. As it's important to check-in regularly with your less developed biological selves, it's likewise essential to do the same with these parts, these Dark Counselors.

We call them "counselors" because they serve you in this capacity. They counsel you. To them, their very existence and survival require they maintain this role in your present and future life. But your growth and healing require that you no longer allow this. You and only you must drive the car. Letting them do it will most certainly result in an accident.

The more you grow and change, the more they'll fight and resist you. These parts of you experience your growing and evolving with dread. In your growing and changing, they see their very existence in jeopardy. They'll fight very hard and will use every means available to hold you back. In truth, they're not dying but instead transforming into higher resonances. But they will not see it this way. They're going to be desperate and terrified of your growth.

Once you engage with and sustain a resonance, in this case, each of your Dark Counselors, it becomes a part of you; it seeks to grow and survive. As such, you must attend to it with patience, love, and acceptance. Never accept what they are and do, but always recognize and accept them as parts of yourself. Since you fed them attention, and thus sustained their lives, you're responsible for their healing and eventual transformation.

What they are today will not be the same in your future. As you evolve and become more, they likewise evolve with your changing resonance. Remember, when two waves meet, the higher wave (you) will lower, or the lower wave (Dark Counselors) will lift, or they'll meet somewhere in-between. When you lift their resonance, in time, they'll transform to become your Light Counselors, but not without a fight.

The Higher Resonances of the Dark Counselors

* Negative Ego - Positive Ego.

* Martyr - Magic.

* Rage - Outrage.

* Shame - Self-Acceptance.

* Control - Love.

* Chauvinist - Awakened feminine energy within you, be you male or female.

As they evolve, they'll eventually die to their darker side and transform into their lighter, like a phoenix emerging from its ashes. These higher resonances, now a part of you, will elevate your growing beyond what you can yet fathom.

By listening to their calls, by attending to their fear and dread, by patiently being present with their raging and panic, you transform them; you help them evolve. The result will be a state of true self-love and true self-acceptance.

Let your Dark Counselors take a personified form when working with them meditatively. It would be interesting to see how they appear to you. Remember, you're not trying to change them. Change must be organic. It must be in its own time and in its own way. You're there to listen, love, and reassure them. You attend to them meditatively so you won't have to deal with their rage and fear in the form of life's many crises and whirlwinds. They'll get your attention one way or another. I recommend giving them your attention meditatively.

Your outer reality is an out-picturing of your inner reality. Attend meditatively to the whispers and shouts of your many biological selves, and the fears and wailings of your Dark Counselors, and you won't have to deal with them in your outer experiences. It's much easier that way.

Essential Points to Consider When Attending to Your Developing Selves and Dark Counselors

When attending to your younger selves and Dark Counselors, be mindful that there are ways you should approach your work with them. Success will depend on how you respond to them and by knowing what your intentions are in engaging them. Some of your parts will be unpleasant, some less so. Engage them not as a scornful parent but as a loving and patient friend and guardian. There are things you should do and things you should not do to aide in their healing and growth. There are ways to work and behaviors you must avoid.

* Don't become angry or impatient with your younger selves or Dark Counselors. Be understanding and forgiving at all times.

* The 'you' you were as an infant is not the same as you at 2, or 5, or 6, or 16, or 18, etc. Each part of you has different experiences, different hurts and pains, and different needs and wants. Don't treat them the same. Allow them their differences.

* Always be loving and attentive no matter how angry or enraged they are with you. Learn to listen. Cultivate empathy.

* Don't rush or expect them to change according to your pace; they must always be allowed to grow and evolve at the pace that's most comfortable for them. Working with your lesser developing selves is a lifelong process; rushing them and being hard on them is rushing and being hard on yourself. Always avoid this. Remember, these parts are you!

* Listen to them; don't lecture them.

- Catch yourself when you're becoming angry or annoyed; they'll feel your resonance; they'll feel cut off and abandoned by you their future. You're alienating these parts by your negative feelings toward them. You're there to respond to their fears and fits of anger. You're there to reassure them that they're going to be protected by you. You're there to offer them love and support. Don't abuse them. Remind them with sincerity that they're loved and supported. Assure them that you'll respond whenever they call out to you. Be the loving and supportive future that you desire for yourself. When you do this, you'll awaken self-love, and everything will change for all of you.

- Always be sensitive to their feelings. Let yourself feel what they're feeling. Never forget that these younger selves are you. You're going nowhere without them. Their healing is your healing; their growth is your growth.

- The happier you become, the more successful you become, the more awakened you become, and the more elegantly your life unfolds, the more fearful and angry the various parts of you will be. Remember, in their time and space, such feelings and elevated experiences are unknown or calibrated differently. As such, these experiences are terrifying to them. For example, your experience of greater love resulting from your growing and maturing is different from what they believe love to be from their limiting and often painful experiences. For some, love may equate with sacrifice or loss. For some, love may equate with pain and abandonment. For some, it may be akin to violence and abuse. As you awaken more love in your life, your younger selves will feel a sense of sacrifice or loss, pain or abandonment, or violence or abuse, etc. They experience the higher resonance of love, but it's calibrating through their limited receptors of dark and painful experiences. They'll need more attention and more patience. They'll need reassuring that they're not being abandoned. They'll need time to grow their receptors.

* When times are going well, take time to pause to let your younger selves catch-up; when times are not going well, check-in and give them attention.

* Stop believing that your less developed selves are holding you back. Stop blaming them because your life's not unfolding as quickly or as elegantly as you'd like. You're all journeying together, though in different times and spaces, and at different resonances. You must never allow yourself to race too far ahead of them. You'll need to pause and wait for them to catch up; this is self-pacing. Pacing yourself is essential on any journey.

* Promise that you'll always be there when they need you, and always keep your promise. Listen and respond to their many whispers and shouts.

* Cultivate in you the patience of your more developed self. It will be a valuable aid in your work of healing and attending to the lesser of you. Think about how patient your Higher Self and God and Goddess are with you.

* Your Dark Counselors are not creative, but they're very persistent. They use the same methods of holding you

back over and over again. Learn to identify their patterns and routines. Watch for them in your reality, and when discovered, don't allow them to be at play.

* Respond meditatively to your younger selves and Dark Counselors. Respond when you feel in the doldrums and when unpleasant emotions surface. Respond when your life becomes chaotic and when you're in a crisis. Respond when you feel overwhelmed. And respond when your life is racing so fast that it requires you to slow down to let the less developed parts catch-up. Even when times are good, and success and happiness abound, go into meditation and check-in; your lesser selves need time to integrate these positive times. As instructions for cold relief medication tell you, '*Take at the first sign of a cold,*' meditate at the first sign that something is not right in your reality. Learn to catch the whispers. Be conscious.

* If you're younger selves are fearful, they'll do whatever it takes to get your attention. Don't worry that you'll be unable to work with them. They're desperate to get your attention. They want you to hear and to respond to them. They're calling out to you always. It's better to address their fears proactively than to have your reality force your attention. If you're having difficulty relating to them, or hearing their cries, or communicating with them, it's due to you, not them. It's your fear, or anger, or wanting to disconnect from them that's standing in the way. Process this, ask for help from your Higher Self, and release it.

CHAPTER 15

Growing Your Spirituality

*Deepen and expand your spirituality.
Let it have life and value in you.
Let it become a priority.
In time, it will become your only priority.*

Spirituality is one's relationship with that
which is more than oneself.

We all have spirituality, even atheists and agnostics. Spirituality is a relationship, not a belief. Some relationships are ugly, some beautiful; some are expressed violently; some reveal themselves in acts of love and kindness. Some are distorted and limiting, some free of distortion and ever-expanding.

Spirituality for some was born of abuse and pain; for others, love and compassion. For some, it forged out of hatred and fear.

For some, it sprang from a deep connection with the wonder of All That Is. Each of us has a different relationship, a unique and personal relationship.

Your spirituality is a reflection of your relationship to 'that which is more than yourself,' not the other way around. The relationship God/Goddess/All That Is has with you is transcendent and always expanding. It's what you bring to the relationship that determines the nature, dark or light, of spirituality for you. Each person's spirituality is an expression of the complexities of his or her connection to God/Goddess/All That Is, their Higher Self, their Soul and Spirit, and their Future Self.

For an atheist, the relationship is one of denial; for an agnostic, it's one of confusion and uncertainty. For those in most religions, the relationship is one of subservience, struggle, martyrhood, sacrifice, and pain; for an enlightened few, it requires nothing but a willingness to love and be loved; no struggle, martyrhood, sacrifice, or pain required. For most, it's born of a child's projection of mother and father; for a few, it's a pursuit of glorious Oneness. What is your relationship, and what do you add of your beliefs and needs and wants? Do you want a relationship that 'gets you something' or a relationship that 'leads you somewhere,' that nurtures your becoming?

You can discover your spirituality in religion, that's true, but you'll never find religion in spirituality. When two or more people attempt to structure shared tenants with set beliefs and fixed dogmas, each individual's unique connection and relationship is constricted and limited. When two or more people share the same spirituality, the same relationship, religion is born. One's spirituality, one's individually unique connection, becomes fixed and often imprisoning.

God/Goddess/All That Is love no one more, no one less, and no one the same. Their love for each of us is unique. Their relationship with each of us is personal and always expanding. And there's nothing you can do that will make them love you more, and nothing you can do that will make them love you less.

Respect your religious heritage. It's a valuable part of the backdrop of who you are. But at some point, you'll need to free yourself from the restrictions of its tenants and beliefs and discover and hone the unique spirituality that flourishes in the complexity of the grander 'you' you're becoming; that you, that Being of Light that shines radiantly in your future.

Stop trying to squeeze the 'you' you're becoming into the old templates of the past; you will not fit. You're expanding in all ways. Stop trying to make sense of this expansion by adjusting it to old beliefs and limiting dogmas. Your need to do so is born of fear and control. Such attempts will not advance you.

Be you a Christian, Muslim, Jew, Hindu, Buddhist, atheist, agnostic, or something else, or none of the above, move beyond to the uniqueness of an ever-evolving connection that transcends all beliefs and rituals. In so doing, you'll discover more of yourself and deepen more of your spiritual relationship. And you'll awaken more of your sense of freedom and oneness.

It would be of benefit to know your current relationship with that which is more than you. It would be wise to process and question what you hold this connection to be; how you view this relationship? For example,

Do I expect God and Goddess to be a father and mother?

Do I see my role in this relationship as that of a child, sinner, or something less and inferior?

Do I deny that I even have such a relationship?

How did I come to this relationship? Who were my teachers?

What was I taught?

Does this relationship expand or contract me, and why?

Process everything about that relationship; leave no belief unchecked, no aspect of it unobserved. Now question your relationship; question everything about it. Love pays attention to detail. Love continually seeks to expand and surpass itself. Ask yourself, *"Does my relationship nurture my becoming more, or does it keep me fixed and unwavering?"* Process and continue processing. Always reach and allow for the complexities of the relationship. Never attempt to figure it out; you'll not be able to. Reach and keeping reaching, lift, and be ever lifted.

Growing your spirituality should become a priority. In time, it will become your only priority, for within a secure and ever-growing and expanding spirituality lies the power to carry you all the way Home. Within your ever-evolving relationship lies the truth of you, the healing of you, and the oneness and wholeness you have for lifetimes sought. In your connection to that which is more than you lies your freedom and your goodness, truth, and beauty.

Spirituality is not necessary for healing, but it becomes necessary if you wish to move beyond the need for healing. Spirituality is not a requirement for your growth, but it becomes so if you want to elevate your growing beyond what you can do on your own. You can go only so far in your becoming. A time will come when you'll need to be lifted. Now would be an excellent time to deepen and elevate your relationship. I'm just suggesting.

Your Future Self

You have an infinite number of future selves. The ones you align with are attracted by the resonance you're holding. Lift your resonance, and you attract futures reflective of your growth. Lower your resonance, and you attract futures reflective of your fear.

By pursuing, by being more aware of, and by being more accepting of your beauty, truth, and goodness, you align with the future that resonates with that elevated state, and you align with your Future Self who resides there.

Meet this Future Self. Let it be a friend and guide. No, it won't tell you what stocks to buy or to avoid someone named Alice. It will not short-cut your growth, for it understands the process needed to become it. But it will love and support you and help with your growing and changing. And when you one day become it, you'll remember having met and having worked so wonderfully together. When you become your Future Self, then you can meet its Future Self.

Your Higher Self

You're a part of your Higher Self; your Higher Self is a part of you. No, your Higher Self is not *"Your Higher Power."* Be careful of the terms you use. Your Higher Self is not superior to you or better than you; it's not a big Energizer Bunny; it's not a super-powerful battery. It's more than you, that's all. All your many lifetimes past, and lifetimes yet to be, have the same Higher Self. It was your Higher Self who created all of you, knowing that one among you will choose to Come Home.

Your Higher Self never has been and never will be physical, but it will assume a personified human form in the meditations you do together. Whatever personified form it chooses, it will be for your comfort and ease of interaction. No, it will not take the form of a rabbit, as one of my clients wanted to make it. Your Higher Self is not Roger the Rabbit, or Jiminy Cricket, or the Mad Hatter, or Princess Leia, or any other such nonsense. This foolishness is the minimizing work of your negative ego. Allow your Higher Self to take whatever form it takes and let it be consistent. It may appear to you in the same or opposite gender, and it will appear around your age or slightly older. But it will not look at all like you.

We recommended that you grow and prioritize this relationship. Your Higher Self does not require you to do so; it does not require anything of you or from you, but your journey of becoming will be infinitely more elegant and expanding through its guidance, love, and friendship. Your Higher Self will never lie to you or demand your loyalty or servitude. It will ask nothing of you and expect nothing from you. It merely loves, cherishes, and stands beside you always. Its love for you is beyond all knowing and understanding, and its patience is unending. And it's more real than you.

Like any relationship, start slowly and honor the ebbs and flows. Your Higher Self is there to guide you Home and is there to lift you into the waiting arms of God/Goddess/All That Is.

Your Soul and Spirit

Between your Higher Self and God/Goddess/All That Is, is the luminescent realm of your Soul and Spirit. No, you're Soul and Spirit are not stuck inside you, somewhere around your heart and liver. And, yes, your Soul is within you, but your Soul is also all about you. Your Soul is everywhere. You're a part of your Soul as it's a part of you. Your Soul does not reside in some fixed place. Your Soul and Spirit transcend the limits of time and space and form.

Your Soul, being feminine energy (not female energy), gives birth to your Spirit, masculine energy (not male energy), in each of your many lifetimes. Your Soul never dies, but your Spirit dies when you do. But it's born anew in each new lifetime.

Your Higher Self and your Soul work closely together to guide, to protect, to inspire, and to bring you Home. They're always by you and ever at the ready when you call upon them.

God, Goddess, All That Is

"Goddess created God, and together they created All That Is."
—Lazaris

Attempting to describe or write about the eternal and the ineffable is an act of folly. The only way to make God/Goddess/All That Is real for you is in your relationship with them, not in understanding them, which you'll never be able to do. Let this relationship have an ever-expanding and ever-deepening connection. Your relationship is your knowing; your ever-awakening love your foundation of understanding.

> ***Accept the love of God/Goddess/All That Is.***
> ***It's in their love you'll discover yourself.***

CHAPTER 16

The Golf Course and the River

*Seek the Sacred Hallows of beauty, enchantment,
love and blessed solitude.
There, rest, refit, and replenish yourself
for the journey yet before you.*

Many years ago, I purchased a 23' house-boat I christened the *"Sea Muse."* It was a dream I had all my life. As a young child, I wanted to live aboard a ship and perhaps do a little pirating now and again. As an adult, I now imagined myself powering around the coastal waterways near my home in Rockport on the North Shore of Massachusetts, and maybe do a little pirating now and again. I moored the *Sea Muse* at a marina on the Merrimack River across from beautiful Maudslay State Park. This ship was my Jolly Roger, my HMS Bounty, my Ironsides, my Black Pearl, and I lived aboard her for two glorious summers.

I didn't do an awful lot of pirating; in fact, during those two years I had her, I only took her out on the water twice. But the *Sea Muse* was my muse, my anchor, my safe haven from the rough seas, and the occasional storms and tempests of life. She was my unbreakable connection to Nature and my unwavering link to enchantment. She was my sea muse.

We all need such connections, such links, such anchors, and we all need from time to time a safe harbor to rest, refit, and replenish before once again weighing anchor, and once again embarking on our life's grand adventure.

How wondrous it was to sit atop the *Sea Muse* on a warm summer's evening dreaming of adventures yet to come, and seas needing exploration. How enchanting it was to soar with the eagles high above Maudslay Park and to imagine endless vistas of forested virgin futures and seas teeming with infinite possibilities. How magical it was to swim with the occasional seal up the Merrimack to discover unfamiliar ports.

Atop my floating oasis, I'd see the other boaters scurrying madly about preparing for their morning fishing excursions. And in the evening, after a hectic and tiring day, they'd sit on their decks, drinks in hand, dreaming, musing, and wondering. People are sorely in need of the beauty of Nature, yet some are so uncomfortable within it, they have to give themselves reasons to be there. I think that's why we have such pastimes as fishing and golf.

Some of the most beautiful places you'll come across are golf courses. Yet so many people have this strange need to trudge along pulling heavy bags about or ride in tipsy carts putt-putting about, then stop, whack a little white ball with a stick in some vain attempt to get it into a small hole and then continue onto the next sandpit. All this to justify their presence in beauty. Don't get me wrong; I enjoy occasional golf now and again, just like the next person.

For so many, Nature, with all her beauty, enchantment, love, and blessed solitude, is a frightening and uncomfortable place. Yet we all require of her gifts and blessings as our well-being is linked to her.

Many resist the callings of the real and the sacred, especially in themselves; many fight tenaciously their goodness, truth, and beauty. Becoming more will always be met with much resistance because becoming more is much too revealing. We'd rather retreat in our delusions of grandeur or insignificance. We'd rather hide in our duties and obligations. We'd rather believe the false ego demands for struggle, hard work, and toil, and we'd rather lose ourselves in the many stories we tell ourselves that we're not loved, not valued, and not at one with All That Is. What we require the most, we fear the most. And when in fear, we scatter and hide. We putt-putt about, whack a few balls, cast a few lines, drink a few drinks, and stay busy. If we slow down, even for a minute, heaven forbid, we may meet ourselves face to face, and heaven forbid, love the person we meet.

In C.O.R.E. work, and for that matter, any healing work, the pursuit of beauty is of vital importance. Beauty can be found in Nature, and beauty can be found all about you. You must pursue her, and you must let her pursue you; you must answer her calls, and you must allow her to seduce you. But know that beauty is a hard lover. She'll demand much from you. She'll demand you drop your lies and delusions; she'll demand your realness, she'll demand you cease your pursuit of short-cuts and quick-fixes. She'll demand an end to your false stories of being less-than or more-than, of being unloved and unappreciated, of being flawed and defected. She'll demand to see your beauty, goodness, and truth. And she'll require your undivided attention. But know this; beauty will always give back more than she asks of you. Beauty is among the greatest of healers, beauty will awaken your creativity, and beauty will guide you on your journey of Coming Home. And it's beauty that will carry you to heights beyond anything you can yet imagine. Pursue her always and let her ever seduce you, whether on a river, a golf course, or wherever you may be.

The Sacred Hallows

Upon your journey of becoming more, it will be necessary from time to time to pause for a while in the Sacred Hallows of beauty, enchantment, love, or blessed solitude.

Life ebbs and flows. There are times when you must act (advance), and there are times when you must pause (integrate). This rhythm is necessary for your growth and essential for your younger selves to catch-up with that growth. When you're in such times of ebbing, take a pause and seek either beauty, enchantment, love, or blessed solitude. Although they'll all call out to you, one among them will call the loudest. That place is your Sacred Hallow; that one responds most to your resonance.

Flowing does not mean over-doing it; even activity needs pacing. And ebbing like-wise does mean burning yourself out.

How many vacations end in serious fatigue and debilitation? Ebbing doesn't mean you play two rounds of golf, battle that two hundred pound tuna, and then get drunk; it also doesn't mean sitting around and doing nothing. Ebbing is a time for processing and programming, a time to assess and re-assess, and a time to rest and renew. And, most importantly, a time to dream futures. Much inner work is none during times of ebbing.

Ebbing and flowing, being and doing, can be very confusing and challenging for some people. 'Doing' is masculine energy; 'being' feminine energy. Both must be in balance for health, well-being, and growth. But men often have difficulty with the idea and execution of 'being.' They simply find 'being' too hard to 'do.'

It's Thursday night. Betty and Bob are sitting at the dining room table. Bob asks Betty, *"Hey, dear, what do you want to do this weekend?'*

Betty replies, *"I don't know, honey, why don't we just hang-out and just be together for a change?"*

(A long pause)

Bob speaks, *"But what do you want to do while we're being together?"*

"I don't know, honey ... just ... you know ... be together," replies Betty. *"Let's just see what happens."*

(Now there's an even longer pause. Bob is perplexed as to what to do.)

Poor Bob. With his over-abundance of masculine energy and his lack of balance with his feminine, Bob finds it hard to simply 'be.'

Taking the time to enter your personal Sacred Hallow and to allow its power to nurture and re-charge you is strongly advised. Where do you find beauty? Where or what do you do to discover enchantment? Where is love's embrace for you? And in what places do you find that oh so amazing blessed solitude? And which Hallow touches you the most? Answer these for yourself?

When life gets choppy, and the winds of change become chaotic and unyielding, pull into your Safe Harbor and rest awhile. Go deep within yourself and let Nature work her magic.

The following are just a few of the blessings and gifts the Sacred Hallows will bestow.

* You'll awaken and discover so much more of yourself there.

* You'll enliven and renew your creativity and the power of innovation.

* You'll receive deep and profound healing.

* You'll find the answers you seek, and insights into life's mysteries and secrets.

* You'll stir the sacred cauldrons of mystery and magic, and invite the healing gifts the Ancient Ones provide.

* You'll open yourself to magical synchronicities and invite enchanted moments.

* You'll hear more clearly the voice of your Higher Self and feel more completely the embrace of God/Goddess/All That Is.

* You'll be present, in such places, with your beauty, truth, and goodness.

* You'll become refreshed, renewed, replenished, and reinvigorated to once again engage in your great adventure of becoming more.

* And you'll soar with eagles and imagine endless vistas of forested virgin futures and seas teeming with infinite possibilities, and perhaps do a little pirating now and again.

You dream in your Sacred Hallow, perhaps its most blessed gift and promise. Dream, dream, and never cease your dreaming. It's how you'll make your future happen.

PART 3

ASAT™ C.O.R.E. Counselors: Your Guides and Cheerleaders Along the Way

CHAPTER 17

ASAT C.O.R.E. Counseling

*If you desire better client's, always become more
and never let go of the pursuit of your
beauty, truth, and goodness;
for a healer will never allow a client to go deeper
then he or she is willing to go themselves.*

What percentage of the population do you believe has some form of a mental health issue? I've had people answer anywhere from 50% to 100%. The truth, according to the National Alliance on Mental Illness (NAMI), is roughly 1 in 5 US adults experience mental health issues each year. Since 20% of the population will require the services of licensed mental health professionals, that leaves 80% who do not. Where do they go for help with everyday life issues and difficulties? Since they're not ill, why seek out the services of those specializing in illnesses?

For generations, the mental health and psychological communities have convinced the public that everyone could use, or should use, their services, since, according to them, everyone has or will develop at some point some form of mental health issue. To their credit, that's good marketing. But it's not true. 20% genuinely have mental health problems needing the intervention of licensed professionals; the remaining 80% face life problems and challenges but do not always require mental health intervention.

Many years ago, *Psychology Today* magazine sent out a questionnaire to former and current patients of psychologists and other mental health professionals. They wanted to get their impression of the work undertaken. Over 90% of respondents replied that even though they felt benefits from the services, they none-the-less felt as though they were *"going around in circles"* concerning the issues needing attention.

Not everyone requires the same approach to healing, as not everyone comes from the same place in their needs and growth. Some people are expanding the boundaries of their living in ways that require a different focus and a different set of tools and perspectives. Many are seeking, consciously or unconsciously, a life of magical synchronicities, a life of greater freedom, and a richer and more vibrant quality of life marked by deeper self-awareness, an awakening of their truer nature, and a greater self-clarity and elegance. Many are growing and becoming in ways that far exceed the services of those trained only to handle disorder, illness, and psychological pathology. Such clients are not sick; their evolving. And this is where ASAT™ C.O.R.E Counseling comes in.

ASAT™ C.O.R.E. counselors are not doctors, psychiatrists, psychologists, clinical social workers, etc. They do not treat, prescribe, or diagnose anything. They're members of a unique and distinct profession that provides a valuable service that mainstream professionals are untrained to provide. They're grounded in a metaphysical approach and a kind of spirituality that transcends religious forms and structures. They're trained to address the needs of those navigating through monumental evolution and change.

ASAT™ C.O.R.E counselors address the blockages and barriers that often restrict and impede one's unique journey of becoming more. A client may be enmeshed in struggles and difficulties and challenges we all face in the day to day living of life, but, as the saying goes, *"If it walks like a duck, and quacks like a duck, it's a duck."* Well, not always. Sometimes it's not a duck. The resistances and impedances of one who journeys a path of profound growth and change do not spring from the same source as others; and, as such, require a different intervention.

ASAT™ C.O.R.E. counselors are guides and fellow journeymen to those who travel a path often wrought with fear and confusion, and resistance. They provide a map, the C.O.R.E map, to help navigate the way and to provide the traveler with invaluable tools, understanding, and guidance, to make the traveling more comfortable, more enjoyable, more steady, and more magical. Unlike others in the healing arts who are not trained for such work, the ASAT™ C.O.R.E. counselor provides aid and comfort to those in need of its unique form of healing and can illuminate a road that's often dark and fearful; a road traveled only by a very few. They are highly qualified in the profound work they do, for they, too, are fellow travelers on the path of becoming more; this does not make them special, only different.

ASAT™ C.O.R.E. Counseling is a unique profession with unique individuals engaged in it. And each counselor adds a wonderful unique flavoring to the mix. Many incorporate other modalities in their healing practice, but all are grounded in the C.O.R.E. principles.

ASAT™ C.O.R.E. Counseling provides each client with the insights, tools, and practice to allow them, in time, to become their own counselor and their own healer, the ultimate triumph of the C.O.R.E. work.

Notes for the ASAT™ C.O.R.E. Counselor

* ASAT™ C.O.R.E. counselors must have well defined and elevated principles and possess the integrity to adhere to them.

* Never diagnose, treat, or prescribe. Such things belong to the domain of those trained and licensed to perform them. Don't pretend to be a doctor, psychiatrist, or psychologist. Don't be something you're not. If you want to be such things, get the necessary education and license. If you're going to be an ASAT™ C.O.R.E. counselor, do only what you were certified and trained to do.

* Journey the path of becoming more. What good are you to your clients if you don't do the work yourself? That's like teaching someone tennis without ever picking up a racquet.

Be an inspiration, set an example, and from your experience with C.O.R.E. work, know what you're talking about. What you've learned in the training class stays in the class; it's you who must give it life in you.

* Never directly or indirectly attempt to influence, guide, or in any way interfere with the choice(s) a client makes. Your area of focus should be on the 'why' behind the choice(s), not on the choice(s) itself.

* Never buy into a client's fear story, or waste your time discussing it. Don't give truth to a myth. The story's not real; it's not what's happening. The story is what they believe is happening; that's true. Pursue the foundations of the story instead. And address that part of the client who's authoring it and believing the distortion. Discover why?

* In each session, address what needs attention at present. Don't continue where you left off from previous sessions, as things have changed since then.

* Never begin a session with techniques. Counsel the client first. Without processing and programming, no technique will ultimately be successful in affecting healing, growth, and change.

* Your client will always tell you where and what to explore, even though they're unaware of doing so. And they'll always tell you right up front. Cultivate the art of listening beyond a person's words. It's not the story, or what they say, that will show you where to look; It's mostly what they don't say where you'll find what's truly up. Learn to listen and to use your

vast body of knowledge and experience, and to lean on the infinite guidance of your client's Higher Self and yours.

* When a client feels that not much of consequence has occurred since you last talked, and believes that he or she has little or nothing to talk about, know that such sessions will prove to be the most powerful. What needs attention is just lying beneath the surface, ready to spring forth. It will emerge when you ask the client to take a moment to quiet his or her self and just feel the feeling that comes up.

* At the conclusion of each session, always ask how the client is feeling. Make sure they're experiencing an elevated shift in their feelings before they leave.

* Never become seduced by a client's distractions. Always identify which of the 4 D's is present. Such resistance will occur when the client is frightened. Stay focused on surfacing the issue triggering the fear. Your job is not to be liked, or to be enabling; it's to facilitate healing.

* Advertising and expensive marketing do not attract clients to you; your resonance does, along with the help of your Higher Self and the Higher Selves of your clients. If you lack clients, it's because you're blocking the door, not allowing them in.

* Speak to your client, never down to them. Keep your focus high and on point, never adjust your focus to the fears of your client. The client must reach; the therapist must never lower.

* You're a professional. Conduct your practice and design your healing space to reflect that. Stay away from passing out

cookies and milk, and from burning incense that smells like cow poop, and from sacrificing chickens. You're not Mother Sunshine, you're not some Buddhist monk, and you're not a Voodoo priest or priestess.

* Never allow yourself to be seduced or manipulated by a client. Out of fear, they'll attempt to do so. Always stay focused and keep on the task before you.

* Identify the fear responses: the 4 Ds, and others. Unless you do, you'll lose control of the session. When you pick-up fear in your client, stop. Help the client identify and release it. Never rush by it, or avoid it.

* Whatever a client brings to a session, whatever's up for them, there's always a payoff involved. No one ever does what they don't want to do, and they always do what they want to. They may be suffering and begging for release, but the payoff they get is more important, or the issue wouldn't be there. Pursue the secret payoff, the hidden benefit, and bring it their attention, after which it's the client's choice if they want to continue it or not.

* Let your work be fun and uplifting. If it's not, you're inviting your martyr to the sessions. Process this and stop inviting it. If you think you're special and oh so valuable, you're inviting your negative ego to the sessions. Stop this and stop inviting it. Only you and your Higher Self should be there, and of course, your client and his or her Higher Self. If you're still burning out, you should pursue another profession.

CHAPTER 18

The 4 Ds

*On the other side of your primal fear
hiding deep in secret places,
freedom waits, twinkling and sparkling
in the glow of your beauty, truth, and goodness.*

Fear is our first and last emotion. It was born of our separation from God/Goddess/All That Is, and it ends as a final healing gift from our Threshold Guardians. It's a doorway we all pass through to our ultimate healing, and it's a doorway we all pass through when returning, once again, to the loving and eternal embrace of God/Goddess/All That Is. It's our last threshold and our final rite of passage before Coming Home.

All clients respond with fear to the work of healing, whether through mainstream or ASAT™ C.O.R.E. Counseling, for healing requires going into dark and hidden places each of us dreads to enter.

The Unknown is the most powerful of fear triggers. And since dying to our old self to make way for the unknown of the new is a part of the work of ASAT™ C.O.R.E. Counseling, fear is very much inherent in our process. And fear is very much a sign of one's progress.

The goal of healing is not to eliminate fear; we can't. Fear is a natural human emotion; it serves us in our living. But it is a condition of our healing that we transcend the ravages of fear and thus free ourselves from its imprisoning and debilitating presence and our hidden dependence on it.

Fear is a gift from our Threshold Guardian. It marks the boundaries of all our plateaus and transitions, and it tempers and strengthens our will to move forward. Accept these gifts of our Threshold Guardians, don't run and hide from them. Fear is a great motivator and an indicator that our healing and becoming more is on course.

We must not succumb to our fears or let them hinder our growth. It's natural to have them, and it's natural to have resistances, but our passage through these fears and resistances is the challenge of our journey. We must meet the challenge head-on and never cower to unseen and unrealized forces.

Fear is the anticipation of pain and suffering from an event that has not as yet occurred. Fear is a myth, a shadow, a bogeyman lurking in the shadows of a possible future occurrence. Fear has no bases in reality. A child's monster hiding beneath its bed is not real. It only becomes real when you discover one hiding there. Until then, the child's fear is only a story, a myth, a fantasy.

It's a part of our healing that we separate what's real from what's not, and since all reality is a myth, a story filled with fears we convince ourselves will happen based on past experiences; we must begin our healing there. We challenge the fantasy; we re-write the story.

Since the future hasn't happened, and since we all create our futures, we can create futures free of past pains and hurts. We can change their myths and stories. We have the power and authority to do so. And we have an abundance of resources and help; the C.O.R.E. map is among many available.

ASAT™ C.O.R.E. counselors do not and cannot empower you. No one can, as each person is already empowered. Each of us received that power from God/Goddess/All That Is; we just choose not to believe or accept it. The C.O.R.E. map can aid us in awakening and accepting our power, and it can serve as a guide for its direction and use.

Use your power to claim your authorship, and use it to re-write your fear stories. Nothing in your future, nothing in the shadows of your imagination, and nothing under your bed can hurt you, or inflict pain unless you place it there to do so. The past is the fear you hide from; the past is the bogeyman of your resistances.

Shine the light of your luminescent consciousness on the darkness of the unknown. Shine your light beneath your bed, and in the closet, and in the shadowy corners of your room. You'll find nothing there but what you projected from the past. You can awaken from your past and present fears by waking up and claiming your authority to change the reality you're presently living; C.O.R.E. will help you with this. When you claim the power you possess, when you discover the power you lost, and when you reclaim the power you've given and give away still, then cast futures, abundant futures, replete with magic, fun, and synchronous events, and futures free from fear.

Every client entering the office of a counselor or therapist will bring fear with them, every one. And every counselor and therapist must identify when the client is in that fear for healing work to progress. If a therapist or counselor cannot identify the signs, and if they do not address the fear, they've lost control of the session.

Everyone responds to fear in one of four ways; through denial, discounting, distraction, and defense - the 4 Ds. The 4 Ds operate in sequence; everyone starts with the denial response and progresses to defense. No one jumps a response. In other words, no one gets defensive without having first denied, discounted, or distracted at some previous point.

Denial: Denial is the first response in the fear sequence. It's an attempt to distance oneself from the fear or the perceived attacker by pretending it doesn't exist, or that it has no basis in truth.

Discounting: Discounting is the second response in the fear sequence. It's an attempt to minimize the nature, the impact, and details of the fear-inducing situation. It's an attempt to make the fear manageable.

Distraction: To distract is the third response in the fear sequence. It's an attempt to change the discussion, to take the attention off the subject or fear, by focusing the attention elsewhere. This response is one most often used by politicians and political 'talking heads.'

Defense: Becoming defensive is the fourth and final response in the fear sequence. When the other three aren't working, one becomes angry, hostile, or violent. The person avoids feeling fear by replacing fear with another emotion; anger.

These responses are not the only indicators of fear. A client looking upward as if in search of an answer is a fear sign. When a client's voice gets higher in pitch, he or she is showing signs of fear. When in fear, people often escape upward into their heads and into their thoughts. They try to figure out the fear or go up and out of their bodies to avoid intense feelings.

Watch for these signs and learn to spot them. Practice every day when talking to loved ones, friends, or associates. Look for them when watching television or listening to another's conversation. You'll always catch them in politicians and almost all political 'talking-heads.' And, most importantly, catch yourself when you find yourself in denial, or discounting, or attempting to distract, or becoming defensive; you're in fear. When you catch yourself, stop the fear response and allow yourself to feel the emotion. Doing so is a part of the healing process.

You may find it beneficial to make a list of the fear responses you're observing. Jot down which of the four you're watching; this is excellent practice in 4D identification. Through daily practice and attention, you will, in time, more easily spot when others are in fear, and most importantly, when you are.

The following is an example of a fear sequence.

A woman suspects her husband of cheating with his secretary, Gloria, and decides to confront him about it.

Wife: John, we need to talk. What's going on between you and Gloria?

Husband: What! What are you talking about? Nothing's going on between us. Whatever gave you the crazy idea that something was? (laughs) – **Denial**

Wife: Mary saw the two of you having dinner last Tuesday when you told me you were out with friends.

Husband: Oh, that! (He laughs again, nervously) Last Tuesday was Gloria's birthday. I was celebrating it with her. It was a birthday dinner. Just trying to be nice, you know me – **Discounting**

Wife: Listen, John, don't lie to me. What's going on!

Husband: (Getting angry) Oh, really! Oh, really! Ok, why don't we talk about the affair you had with Bob when we were dating! Why don't we talk about that! – **Distraction**

Wife: No! That was then, and this is now. Stay on the subject!

Husband: Oh, yeah! Oh, yeah! (Huffing and puffing, he storms out the room and slams the door behind him) – **Defense**

CHAPTER 19

Three Clients

Healing results from the client's choice to heal.
The therapist can either inspire or hinder that choice;
and that's all they can do.

Not all clients approach healing from the same place. All therapists are aware of this.

As a healer, knowing the clients you're dealing with and what it is they expect from you will significantly enhance the work you do and the results achieved. You wouldn't address a sore tooth by attending to a toe; unless you're an acupuncturist (just kidding).

Almost all therapists approach clients as if they're a single homogenous group, all seeking the same result; healing. This thinking is far from correct. Although most clients seek an end to pain and suffering, many seek something more. And what they seek more is what they get, and that's not healing. Some seek attention, and some seek an audience to hear their dark story; some seek to validate their suffering, some seek quick fixes, some seek an enabler, some seek approval, and, yes, some seek true healing. Without understanding the various underlying agendas of their clients, therapists can become frustrated, see themselves as failing, become tired and drained, and sometimes grow to be insensitive and uncaring. Knowing what your client expects and what he or she is willing to give or not give to the work at hand will make your undertaking more effective and less draining.

There are three levels of clients a therapist will face in their practice. Knowing each will help you navigate the terrain of their resistances and expectations. Of the three levels, some seek attention more than healing, some look to cure only, and some will have the willingness and courage to invade their privacy for healing to occur. Study the following levels and learn to identify them. Don't judge them; accept and understand them. In doing so, you can help them advance.

(1) The Get-Bys: No matter what healer this client goes to, or what healing procedure he or she chooses, this client will not take the responsibility required for healing to happen. The Get-Bys are life's victims, or so they erroneously believe, and it's up to others to take responsibility for them; after all, they're the ones who are suffering and need the most help, don't you see? To them, healing is about getting attention. With a few exceptions, this group does not want the pain and suffering in their lives; this is true. However, what they want more then healing the pain and suffering is the attention that the pain and suffering provide, the attention they so desperately seek. They use their pain and suffering to get that attention. For this group, attention equates to love.

> *"I'm suffering! If you love me, you'll help me!
> You're the healer; it's your responsibility to help me!"*
> They'll cry out, tearfully

> *"But what about helping yourself?"* You ask.

> *"Oh no, I can't! I can't! I'm suffering!"* They reply,
> *"I'm too much in pain! I need you to do it!"*

Their life is a get by, one day at a time affair. Theirs is a life with no future; it's the sad existence of just getting by. As a healer, there's not much you can do for them. If you were to make their lives more comfortable, it would not fit in with their secret template of pain and suffering as a means to gain attention and therefore love. They'll eventually sabotage the effort. The Get-Bys are the smallest of the three groups, but the clear majority of the country's wealth, and the healer's focus and energy, is on them. They're the 'attention-getters.'

(2) The Move-Ons: This client will take some degree of responsibility. They will, for the most part, cooperate with their therapist's suggestions and treatment options. They'll take the pills, attend the sessions, undergo the operation, and do all that's required to move on with their lives. But don't dare ask them to go into their dark and hidden places where true healing is needed. That's a line they'll not cross. For the Move-Ons, healing is fixing the problem only. For them, pain and suffering is a temporary setback. *"Fix the problem so I can move on with my life."* Sure, they can cure cancer or whatever problem they're experiencing, but the condition is only an out-picturing of the unconscious issue in need of attention. Unless healed, it will emerge again, in the same or a different form, in this lifetime or another.

These dark and hidden places hold an intense level of pain that requires its feeling for healing to happen. And although the Move-Ons feel deep and frequent emotions, they'll not allow themselves to experience the deeper emotions to the full extent required for releasing them. As such, they cannot move beyond them. What emotions they feel are safe emotions for them. It's one thing to be emotional; it's another to plunge deep into the emotion to discover and retrieve the power hidden in its depth. The pain, the rage, the dread, etc. will not be released until the power they hold is brought back and made a part of them once again; this is the good news.

What the Move-Ons will not let in is that as they invade their emotional privacy, they become free of the pain, the hurt, the rage they've stored so deeply. There's tremendous power in our hidden emotions, a power that can create magnificent futures of healing, magic, and dreams manifested. This power can catapult one to the heights of unimagined freedom. The Move-Ons are the largest and most common of the three groups.

(3) The Move-Beyonds: This group will take responsibility. Their choice is no longer to get-by or move-on. They're in this life to move beyond; they're not here to patch-up or repair their current vehicle; they're here to discover a whole new mode of transportation. Unlike the Move-Ons, they'll invade their hidden and forbidden dark places and discover the incredible power lost there, and they'll bring that power back to make it apart of themselves once again; and they'll succeed for the whole universe is there to help. However, it's important to note that the Move-Beyonds will put up the most fight and offer the most resistance during this process. They're going into the unknown of themselves and are willing to risk the most in doing so. They'll be the most frightened, but they'll succeed in their pursuit. And your work together will be glorious and magical.

It's ironic that the attention so desperately sought by the Get-Bys, and the safety so rigidly needed by the Move-Ons, are available to the Move-Beyonds in unlimited supply. Fear is the limiter of the first two groups; responsibility the liberator of the third. All are loved, supported, and offered help. Still, it's only the third group that chooses to take responsibility and exercise the courage to be willing to receive it and to allow the receiving to occur.

The Move-Beyonds are moving beyond their old templates and current set to discover the incredible majesty of their future. And what a magical and marvelous journey it will be for them.

Because our world is in the midst of monumental change, this group is the smallest but fastest-growing. The times require it.

The Move-Beyonds require another kind of healing and a different type of healer to help them on their journey, for not all healing approaches, and not all healers can provide what they need; this is where C.O.R.E comes in. The healers they require must be Move-Beyonds themselves: ASAT™ C.O.R.E. counselors.

We should note that each level will progress in sequence. Get-Bys will eventually mature and advance to become Move-Ons; they'll not jump directly to Move-Beyonds, however. It would be too frightening for them to do so. And, of course, Move-Ons will change and advance to become Move-Beyonds.

Some therapists choose to work only with a particular group. Often people possessing the most developed hearts and the most awakened compassion gravitate to the first group, the Get-Bys. This choice is a beautiful choice, since love and compassion are potent motivators. Who best to motivate Get-Bys to reach for curing more than requiring attention, and Move-ons to strive for healing despite their fear and need for secrecy? But remember, be careful not to become seduced into enabling the problem. Many clients will attempt to manipulate those with ungrounded love and compassion.

Each group has different needs and different expectations, and working with them requires an abundance of patience, love, self-discipline, and focus, and most certainly an understanding of who and what you're dealing with.

Never buy into the neediness of the Get-Bys; doing so enables their hidden agenda of getting attention. Your empathy, sympathy, and caring are not for their victimhood, but their suffering, pain, and humanity. Always approach Get-Bys by expecting more from them. Inspire in them the pursuit of curing; treat them as if they're Move-On's.

Never buy into the fear and reluctance of the Move-Ons. Your empathy, sympathy, and caring are not for their refusal to go deeper, but for their terror and anguish in doing so. Always expect more from them; work with them as if they're Move-Beyonds.

C.O.R.E is the work for Move-Beyonds; it serves them better. Although they'll resist you the most, and will put up the greatest fight, they'll succeed in their healing; it's what they came into this life to do.

If you wish to attract Move-Beyonds to your practice, you must be one yourself; otherwise, you've nothing to offer this group. They'll not waste their time with you. They're moving forward; you're choosing not to.

Be patient with them and always stay focused on the 'how's' and 'whys' of their reality creation. Keep your attention on their limiting raw materials, and the whispers and shouts of their many parts of self and dark counselors. And always treat them as fellow travelers on your separate paths of becoming more.

CHAPTER 20

The Hidden Killers

There's nothing you do in life that you don't want to do,
And there's nothing you don't do that you want to.
Search the secret places within you
and you'll discover this to be true.

Death is not the result of failure. Although many in the healing professions, and those wedded to consensus thinking, believe it is. Such erroneous beliefs and thinking should never be entertained by those entrusted with our care and healing. Death may be the conclusion to a particular life's journey, but it's never the end of the journey. Our journey has no end.

Death is a natural transition, a blessed doorway between one adventure and another. We should never hold the belief that death is a failure, a punishment, or the consequence of an errant life. We fear the unknown, and death is the most fearsome unknown. But in reality, death is not something new to us since we've done it many times before. We just forgot we did it.

How we live, not how we die, is the only subject worth pursuing, for how we live determines the 'why' and the 'how' of our dying. The grace and dignity of our passing is the measure of a successful passage. And it's in grace and dignity that a successful life is measured. A successful life is one that became more; a wasted life is one that settled for less.

There's no limit to what can end a life, but the cause of death is only the means of passing. The real source of dying is not written in an autopsy report; it's written in a place deeply hidden in each of us. It's discovered in secret places within our unconscious, and it shadows us in the lies we tell ourselves and the false stories we call reality.

Our Hidden Killers are born of the belief in our separation and thrive on the secret agendas and the lies we hold as truth; lies told to us by our negative ego.

Our passing from one life to another results from the disconnection from what's real and genuine in us. Our hidden agendas, the lies told by our negative ego that we hold as truths, the feeding of our Hidden Killers, all separate us from the source of life; our unbreakable oneness with God/Goddess/All That is. Each Hidden Killer denies us our truth, goodness, and beauty. And without these, we exist in a false story written by a false sense of self.

No, we haven't failed. We can't fail in our ultimate destination, our chosen destiny. But we can take our time, and dilly-dally for awhile. And when we dance and play with the Hidden Killers, we dilly-dally quit a lot. But there are other lifetimes to continue our destined journey of becoming more if we choose to make it so.

There are many Hidden Killers, but the following are the most common and most lethal.

Negative Ego: Among the Hidden Killers, the negative ego is the most troublesome and the most deadly. Your ego came into being at birth to provide information for your interpretation. But instead, you expected it to do the interpreting, a task it cannot do. Over time it came to hate you for this, and now it seeks to destroy you. Your negative ego always lies to you, and when allowed to direct your life, it will ultimately lead you further and further away from your truer self.

If you give a five-year-old the task of driving your car, it will invariably crash it. And, if each time it crashes the car, you blame it for its failure, it will grow to fear and distrust you. Over time, with such repeated abuse, it will come to hate you and eventually wish you dead; this is, in a sense, what we've made of our ego.

The ego's sole purpose is to provide information, not to interpret that information. Interpretation is our responsibility. By refusing to take authorship for all aspects of our reality, we created a powerful and determined nemesis; we created a negative ego.

Since the negative ego always lies to us, we should always pay attention to it and check it when it tries to influence our choices and decisions. One of the main tasks of C.O.R.E. work is to identify the play of the negative ego and to respond by assuming authorship for it, and from that place of authority, exercise the function of interpretation of information. Never hand your reality over to your negative ego; doing so will, in time, kill you.

Martyr: Martyrs are the silent sufferers who need an audience to witness their melodrama of being unloved, unappreciated, or overworked. Martyrhood is among the most prevalent and addictive of the hidden killers. Everyone does it from time to time. If you have children, you've done it. Some, however, make a career of it. Martyrhood is a deadly game we play to control, to get attention, and to manipulate others. This game, this false story of being unloved, over-worked, and unappreciated, blinds us to our realness and pushes away the love of others. When we do not allow love in, we will, in time, perish; for love nurtures longevity. All religions put great value in a martyred life, a deadly mistake for those who buy into it.

Victim: Victims are the vocal sufferers who need an audience to hear their dark story. Unlike martyrs, victims are not quiet or silent. Victims delight in sharing their misery and thrive on the pity and sympathy of others. But, like martyrs, their game, their story, will always attract realities that produce the stuff and conditions of victimhood. And like martyrs, their false story will deny them the use of their power to craft lives of value and worth and success.

Shame: Shame is the feeling and belief that you're flawed, defective, broken, or unworthy. Everyone holds the resonance of shame, everyone. We came to it through each of the four phases of our life: childhood, the first-break time (around 8 or 9), adolescence, and adult years. We adopted the belief in our shame through various means: we were taught it, or we were put into situations we could not emotionally handle, or we came to it through abuse, or we formed shame-based psychic contracts with others.

Shame is a debilitating belief and feeling that denies us any sense of our true worth and value. And without the realization of our worth and value, we drift aimlessly through life, passing the time until we pass on.

But the most insidious part of shame is what we do with it in our adult years; instead of processing it, we dump it on to others.

Denied Dreams and Futures: Denied dreams and futures are the refusal to allow oneself a sense of future, goals, dreams, or visions. Denied dreams and futures are potent killers. Without the pursuit of becoming more, we give up the reason to continue our growing; and without growing, we die. We see this when a person dies not long after the passing of their partner.

"Futures create the present on the backdrop of the past."
– Lazaris.

Without dreams, desires, and visions, there's nothing ahead of us to pursue and reach for; this life ends, and we continue in the next. Always dream, desire, and pursue vibrant, positive futures that will challenge you. Your living requires you to do such things.

Destructive Emotions: Destructive emotions are any emotion, positive or negative, you'll not allow yourself to feel. Feel all your emotions, and feel your emotions cleanly. Cleanly feeling your emotions involves feeling them without the desire to harbor them for further use, or to hurt or punish others. Feel your positive emotions and let them lift you; feel your negative emotions, and choose to release them. When we deny ourselves the full expression of our feelings, dark or light, we live a controlled and limiting life lacking in richness and depth. We deny our realness.

Control and Manipulation: Control is the panic-driven need and attempt to keep love safe. Manipulation is the act and need to get others to do what you want; it's a tool used by control. Control hides love so deeply we're unable to find it. Without the full expression of love, life loses value and meaning. Control and manipulation constrict. And if life is not expanding, it will needlessly end.

Rage: Rage is the highest frequency of anger. As a natural human emotion, rage has opposing values:

1. Enrage (negative) – deep and intense anger, highly charged, that gnaws at, tears down, and eventually consumes its host over time.

2. Outrage (positive) – deep anger, highly charged, that motivates one to change and grow.

By working with rage, a person can transform it into its higher resonance. Where the lower resonance of rage consumes its host, the higher resonance feeds and propels it.

Arrogance and Specialness: Arrogance is the belief in being better or less than others. It's a means some adopt to mask intense feelings of shame and insignificance. Specialness is an ego trap that holds the belief of being better than or worse than others; it's a form of arrogance. Arrogance, with its lie of specialness, keeps one's uniqueness hidden. Specialness is a promise your negative ego repeats over and over again to keep you dependant and imprisoned. When you hold firmly to your arrogance and your belief in your specialness, you blind yourself to the truth of you. You live your ego's false story and live its malicious lies. Remember, your negative ego seeks to destroy you, and if left unchecked, it will.

Judgment and Blame: Judgment is a fear attempt to distance oneself from the object of one's judgment. Blame is the act of placing on oneself or others the source or cause of discomfort as a means of avoiding responsibility. By avoiding responsibility, we avoid accepting the authorship of our life; we pass that authorship to others or leave it to the fickle whims of fate. When we distance ourselves from others (judgment) and distance ourselves from responsibility (blame), we distance ourselves from ourselves. In so doing, we impede our growth and slow or stop our journey of becoming more.

Entitlement: Entitlement is the belief that one is owed whatever one needs or wants due to past hurts, disappointments, and pain. When you hold the belief in your entitlement, you deny the gifts and opportunities life provides and the gifts and the love of God/Goddess/All That Is. Within the ego's lies, and within your choice to resist receiving due to your perceived entitlement, you choose to stand alone and disappointed.

Self-Pity: Self-pity is a non-emotion designed to numb a real emotion. Without feeling that which needs feeling, its healing cannot occur. The deadened feeling is locked away and remains unexpressed.

Psychic Contracts: Psychic Contracts are an unconscious bond that ties one person to another, living or dead. For example, because your father struggled his whole life *"to make ends meet,"* out of love and honor, you'll unconsciously not allow success to be easy for you. You'll struggle *"to make ends meet."* Or, because your father expected you to be successful, and because you hated your father, you won't become successful. These bonds are either formed out of love or forged out of hate. All psychic contracts need to be relinquished or re-written that each life may express uniquely.

Validation and Vindication: Validation is the desperate need to prove you're valid, that you belong. Vindication is the burning need to correct the wrongs done to you in the past, real or imagined. Both validation and vindication imprison the holder in the past. And both deny futures toward which to grow the flourish.

Cowardice: Cowardice is not the opposite of courage as most people believe; cowardice is the refusal to tell oneself the truth. Without opening to the truth of oneself, dark or light, one's growth becomes stifled, and the real reason for living, to become more, is lost.

Chauvinism: Chauvinism is the denial or minimization of the power of feminine energy. Chauvinism distorts perceptions and beliefs due to the over-predominance of masculine energy. This distorting energy castrates the beauty and power of masculine energy in men and devalues the power and presence of feminine energy in women.

It should be noted that masculine energy is not male energy, and feminine energy is not female energy. Every man and woman possesses both, only in different configurations. And every man and woman needs a balance between the two to awaken wholeness and to become more.

Because of chauvinism, men fear the incredible power of feminine energy; because of chauvinism, women distrust it. Because of chauvinism, imagination (feminine energy) is minimized and devalued, and logic and reason (masculine energy) become over-relied on and predominant. And since imagination is the most powerful tool among the three used to craft reality, and since imagination is essential for creativity and innovation, it's diminishing leads to dogma, control, intolerance, violence, and lack of vision and dreams.

According to chauvinist thinking, *"Fire's hot. Water's wet. What you see is what you get."*

The work of C.O.R.E., and that of ASAT™ C.O.R.E counseling, is to identify one's Hidden Killers and to facilitate their healing. C.O.R.E. is a powerful work of healing and growth, and an excellent guide on our journey of becoming more.

CHAPTER 21

Round Trip from Eden: Beyond Healing

You are loved, and you are cherished.
That's really all you ever need to know.
You are loving, and you matter.
That's really all you ever need to accept.

You are loved and cared for beyond anything you can ever imagine and anything you will ever know and understand. You are protected on your journey, and you never walk alone upon it. There are so many who are cheering you on, guiding you forward, and walking hand in hand beside you. When you come to know and allow this, you've reached the promise of C.O.R.E.

There's a life beyond the need to fix and cure, and a life and world no longer in need of changing and healing. It's not a world we're familiar with; it's a life, unlike anything we know or can yet comprehend. Beyond healing and changing exists a transcendent reality beyond all need for suffering and pain, beyond all investments in 'less than' or 'more than,' and all beliefs in struggle and toil, and where happiness, joy, magical synchronicities, and bountiful living are the coin of the realm. Beyond healing and changing is not the end of healing and changing; it is, in fact, just the beginning. But beyond healing and changing is a state of being one with that healing and changing, and of being whole and eternally free within its embrace and promise.

Beyond healing and changing, your journey that has no end, ends. You brush yourself off and revel awhile in the beauty, enchantment, love, and blessed solitude. You pause in the sacred hush and there discover and claim your beauty, truth, and goodness, and then you move on, eternally free, eternally loved and fully accepting of that, and forever whole and one. The C.O.R.E. journey ends there; you do not. You stand up and continue on your way, not fixed, not cured, not changed, not healed, but new. The C.O.R.E. work is over; all work is over. It's time to play now. You've accepted your part in the Sacred Covenant and are Home at last.

The Sacred Covenant: Coming Home

No, you weren't kicked out of Eden, and no, you weren't punished for eating an apple in pursuit of knowledge. And no, you were not, and are not, born of sin. You chose to leave on your own accord. You chose to become more, not better, more. You chose to separate from God, Goddess, All That is. You chose to leave your Eden because you desired to elevate your loving; you chose to love consciously.

Oh, you loved. How could you not? You were conceived in love, you exist in an ocean of love, and love is the very DNA of your being. But to consciously choose love, you have to first separate from it; but to do so is impossible. You can't separate from love, no matter how hard you try. But you could pretend you can. You can make-up and make-believe a story that you did.

A fish in the sea knows nothing of water. Its very existence is water. It's never known anything else but water. Only when you separate a fish from the water can a fish know the source, the element from which it sprang. And if the fish were able to live and thrive outside the ocean, it will, in time, grow to understand more and more, and appreciate more and more, the place from which it came. And, in time, the fish could exercise its acquired freedom to choose to return to the source of its existence or not; this would make for a more enlightened fish, a more highly evolved, more consciously aware fish. The separation was necessary for knowledge to occur: separation allowed the fish freedom to choose between differing worlds.

You made a choice to live and love consciously. Why? Because you wanted to become more. You wanted a grander loving, a more magnificent existence, and a deeper, more heightened connection to your source, your element. What is that source? What is that element? Love, of course. But more-so God, Goddess, All That Is, the source of love itself.

No, you were not sinful for choosing to leave your Eden, your love, your element. You were not bad or wrong for making such a choice. Such a choice speaks to your grace and majesty; it radiates from your beauty, truth, and goodness. You're becoming more because you chose to. You're destined to be more, and you're destined to Come Home because you wish it so. It's your destiny. How can you possibly fail? For all that's destined to be will come to fruition; this is a universal truth.

Before you began on your sacred journey, a promise, a covenant was made between God/Goddess/All that is and you. They promised you freedom, and they promised they'd never leave you, always protect you, and ever to love you. They've kept their promise to you and will for all eternity and a day. Your promise, your covenant with them, is that you'd Come Home. Although you've forgotten your commitment, you will, in time, remember. You're destined to do so. You have thousands of lifetimes to remember, and to return to your promise. It only takes one to make this choice. And since we're on the subject, why not this lifetime? I'm only suggesting.

Coming Home is a choice you'll make. Honoring your covenant is something you're destined to do. It could be why you're here in this lifetime, it could be why you're receiving the calls and whispers you're getting, and it may even be why you're hearing those cries and shouts from your panicked parts of self and your terrified Dark Counselors.

You and all the parts of you are Coming Home together, not at the same time and in the same space. Your younger selves have future selves who call out to them to Come Home. Your Dark Counselors have Light futures they're growing to become. You're all in this Great Adventure together. Not one will be left behind.

No, you weren't sent from Eden to live a life of despair and fear; you chose to leave even though such a separation is impossible. How can you be separate from love or from God/Goddess/All That is? It's the water in which you exist; it's your DNA. But you can create any story you wish, and you can believe anything you want; you have the freedom given you to do so. But know this, your journey has a round-trip ticket. You willed it so.

Becoming More

When you separated from God/Goddess/All That Is, you turned about and perceived where once you'd been. You observed a gap between you and Eden, and it was within this gap, fear was born, and illusions came to be. This gap is not real; it couldn't be; you just believed it so. Fear was your first and most significant emotion; it still is. But the nurturing heart of the Goddess held you lovingly to her, and she's never ceased her embracing. And nothing you do, or do not do, will break the embrace she gives you. It's only in your illusions and lies do you keep yourself from sensing her embrace. But, she knows the truth of you; she holds sacred your beauty, your truth, your goodness, and will gladly return them when you're ready and willing to accept them. She's infinitely patient.

Your Higher Self knows your illusion, with its countless stories you convince yourself are real. Your Higher Self has no investment in your fantasies and stories and is always by your side to lift you out of them when you're ready to move beyond. And it's your Higher Self who's always there for you. And when you're ready, and when you give permission, will guide you back to Her embrace, an embrace that never ceased to be. Thus began a journey of Going Home.

A time will come upon that journey when you'll pause, turn about, and make a choice to stop Going Home and start Coming Home. You have many lifetimes to travel with much to learn and experience along the way. But one lifetime will make a choice, and all lifetimes will turn and follow. Thus begins a journey Coming Home.

Becoming more is not having more. Although your negative ego is always trying to convince you it is. Becoming more is not becoming perfect; nothing that exists is. Becoming more does not mean becoming a better you, a souped-up version, a you with more bells and whistles. Becoming more means becoming more. It's not that complicated.

And becoming more is a never-ending journey. There's no end to 'becoming,' no limit to 'more.' Your negative ego promises endings, but you Higher Self delivers eternity. If you just want quick-fixes and magic bullets, C.O.R.E. cannot help you there. There's much work ahead. But the more you pursue, the more of you will be found, and the lighter your path becomes. In time, ease and happiness replace struggle and pain, the whims of fate give way to magic, and all becomes a splendid adventure filled with light, joy, bounty, and masterful artistry.

Allow C.O.R.E to help you along the way. Let its map mark the road before you, and make your trip magical. It may not be the only map to your destination, but it will undoubtedly be the one that will allow your travels to be more elegant and rewarding.

Always pursue becoming more, and let Coming Home become a priority. If you do this, it will, in time, become your only priority.

You're so much more than you yet know; your real truth, your real story has yet to be written. You're about remembering; your about living an existence you once lived and are destined to live again.

> Enjoy your journey. Maybe someday we'll meet
> in a Sacred Hollow. There we can have a slice
> of watermelon or two. You never know.

APPENDIX ONE
Questions and Answers

Question: ***I've been working with my Dark Counselors of martyr and shame for years now. They still keep coming up in my life. When will I finally be done with them?***

Never. As humans, we love to view reality as a straight line. As such, we think of healing as a straight line with a beginning, middle, and end. Healing doesn't work that way. Healing is a spiral, not a straight line. And it always spirals upward. It always comes back around but never in the same place. Healing elevates; it does not end. The more you work with such things as martyr and shame, the less control they have over you. Martyr and shame will always be present though not in the same place on the spiral.

Think of it this way. Let's say you've successfully stopped smoking. You haven't had a cigarette in a long time. But now and then, you sneak out behind the shed to light up. Ok, no big deal! No, you didn't fail; no, you're not a failure. And, no, you're not backsliding. You had your quick fix, now go on with your life and continue smoke-free. And if now and then you sneak behind the shed, again, no big deal. The point is that even though you healed your smoking habit, the urge to smoke will always be there at some level. The difference is you're controlling it, not it controlling you. You've transcended the urge. You're the author of your reality, not the cigarette. Martyr and shame will always be there. And from time to time, you may slip into them. Don't worry. Catch yourself when you slip up, brush yourself off, and get on with living your life; this is healing.

Question: **I've tried and tried to heal my particular issue. Whatever I do never seems to work. I feel so desperate!**

Be careful of self-pity and desperation. When you're in self-pity and desperation, you create a static that will interfere with the receiving of the healing you desire. Process through the self-pity and desperation first, and then approach your healing with calm resolve. Also, look for the presence of martyr in you. If there, work on that first before you move on to the initial issue. Healing will always be given to you; you just need to be a place of receiving.

Question: *Is C.O.R.E Counseling useful for children and adolescents?*

C.O.R.E.'s work is not really for children or adolescents. They're not yet at the point where they possess the adult level of awareness and responsibility necessary for this work to be most effective. Most grown-ups are not adult enough or responsible enough to respond to this work. The C.O.R.E map is suited more for spiritual adults. Children and adolescents have different needs and requirements. It would best serve them, in my opinion, to have them see a counselor who specializes in children and adolescents. Although I must admit, I've worked with a few in the past, and the results were pleasantly surprising. You see, you never know.

Question: ***I've been working with my younger selves for years, but they still keep plaguing me and coming up in my life. What do I need to do to finally fix them?***

Stop trying to fix them! Stop blaming them! They're a part of you; they are you. They must evolve and grow in their own time and at their own pace. Just keep responding to them and loving them. As God/Goddess/All That Is are infinitely patient with you, be patient with them. Be patient with yourself.

Question: ***Sometimes, it's tough to meditate. I either can't relax because my thoughts are racing or I fall asleep. Is there anything I can do about this?***

What you're describing are symptoms of fear. Ask your Higher Self to help you with this. But there are some things you can do.

Sleeping: Try meditating at a time when you're less likely to be sleepy. Meditating at night before going to bed may not be a good idea. Also, don't meditate lying down. Sit up when meditating.

Too Many Thoughts: Trying to push away the thoughts or fighting against them will just make the matter worse. Don't force the meditation. Stop trying and come back another time when you feel less anxious. Try the technique of Freewriting to open a dialogue with the frightened parts of yourself. Freewriting can also help bring to the surface your fear so you can feel and lift it. You may find Freewriting to be more beneficial for you right now. Later, when you feel less frightened, you can return to meditating. (See *'Freewriting'* in Appendix Two: *Techniques*).

Question: ***I don't have the time to meditate or do much of the work suggested. My time is limited. What else can I do that won't take up much time?***

Time's an illusion. You can have as much time or as little time as you want. It's always your call. If you're too busy to process and meditate, you're too busy. Before you proceed further, I would suggest looking honestly at your priorities. If you find that you're growing is not on the top of the list, you may wish to reevaluate what's really important to you. You may not care much about yourself to change, but do you care enough about someone else to change for them? It doesn't matter what motivates change, only that you're motivated.

Question: ***Since using your book and working on myself, a lot of unpleasant emotions have surfaced, and I'm experiencing a lot of resistance. Is this normal?***

Yep! You're succeeding. There will always be resistance to this work. The more you move forward, the more resistance you'll experience. But you'll find that as you grow, your resistances will be better processed by you. Don't forget to pace yourself. Remember, there'll be times when you'll need to move forward, and times when you'll need to pause and integrate. There'll be times when some of your younger selves will need attention.

Don't force your process. Slow down to allow your less develop selves to catch up. You're not in a race here.

Think of your lesser selves as young children hiking with you on a long mountain trail. There'll be many times when you must pause and wait for them. The worst thing you can do is to run wildly ahead. In your exuberance to reach your goal, don't forget the little ones that follow. You're going nowhere without them. Unpleasant emotions surfacing and resistances occurring is a message for you to slow down, pause, and attend to the various parts of yourself who are feeling abandoned. Pacing is everything on your journey. Responding and always attending to your lesser selves is of the utmost importance.

Question: **I'm undecided whether to get help from a psychologist or an ASAT™ C.O.R.E Counselor. Can you advise me?**

If you're feeling torn between the two, I suggest working with a psychologist first. When, and if, your work ends with them, then look into ASAT™ C.O.R.E Counseling. Go with the mainstream programs first. ASAT™ C.O.R.E Counseling is not a substitute for the valuable and important work they do. When you're ready to move on to a different approach, C.O.R.E work will be there to help.

Question: *Much of what you talk about does not fit into my religious beliefs. Can you help me with this?*

Religion will not fit into where you're ultimately going. In time you'll need to expand your spirituality beyond the confines of religion. Becoming a spiritual adult supersedes and surpasses being a religious one. Remember, although you can find spirituality in religion, you'll never find religion in spirituality. Ultimately your relationship with God/Goddess/All That Is must stand as a personal relationship unfettered by dogma, collective belief, or shared rituals. It must shine in its uniqueness and individuality. You're Coming Home to your Oneness, not your 'group-ness.'

Question: **I'm not a licensed therapist or have any training in counseling, but I love helping people, and I feel drawn to this work. Can I still become an ASAT™ C.O.R.E. Counselor?**

Yep. ASAT™ C.O.R.E Counseling is a different profession; there are no prerequisites, other than being over 21, for becoming one. It's not psychology, psychiatry, etc. To become one of those, you'll need the education and licensing required. Most people take the ASAT™ C.O.R.E Counseling training solely for their own self-healing. Some have elected to make a part-time or full-time profession in the field. Others quietly do their C.O.R.E. healing 'work' helping others in the course of their day to day interaction with them. Most graduates elect to employ their training this way. The form is not what's important. The C.O.R.E map is a guide; if you wish to help others using it, either professionally or otherwise, pay attention to what calls out to you. Follow your heart, never your pocketbook.

Question: **How can I find an ASAT™ C.O.R.E. Counselor to work with?**

Our counselors advertise their services online. You can always use Google in your search. But be aware that anyone can call themselves C.O.R.E. counselors; that doesn't make them ASAT™ C.O.R.E. counselors. Since I'm the only one who trains ASAT™ C.O.R.E counselors, and since the term ASAT™ is trademarked, only those listed as ASAT™ C.O.R.E counselors are certified by me to do this work. All others are fake.

Question: ***This book has been so helpful for me! People need this. How can we get more people interested in the C.O.R.E map?***

First of all, thank you for allowing the book to touch you.

Secondly, no one needs C.O.R.E. work. Many paths will take you Home.

Thirdly, this approach to personal growth and awakening is not for everyone. Very few will appreciate or understand it because this work is not everyone's "cup of tea." It's a unique path not suited for most people.

I wrote this book and designed ASAT™ C.O.R.E. Counseling for a particular reader, and a specific client, people who will most benefit from them. You are such a person, and you've created or allowed it to assist you. You're the author of your life, not a book or a particular map. You make of your life what you will, and you'll create the means to get you to where you're going. So I guess it was you who created or allowed this book, or it wouldn't be in your reality (but I still get to keep the royalty).

It says in the Veda, *"The knowledge of the book remains in the book."* It's you who lift the knowledge out of the book. It's you who give it meaning and value. And it's you who give it life in you.

Thank you for inviting me to be a part of your journey. And thank you for allowing C.O.R.E. to help you.

APPENDIX TWO

Techniques

C.O.R.E. Processing Procedure

1. Whenever your outer experience is in chaos or turmoil, or when you feel angry or fearful, or in any way upset, make a choice to see the person, circumstance, or event triggering it differently. Remember, it's good to feel the emotions coming up, but it's not wise to feed the story you currently believe is real. Separate from what you think is the cause of your discomfort by choosing to do so. Choose to step back and take a pause.

2. At a time and place that's conducive, check-in with yourself. Don't wait too long, however, as the issue up to be healed can slip back into the unconscious. Ask for what needs addressing to come to the surface once again. Be quiet. Be still. Close your eyes. Allow yourself to feel the emotions that will, if you're not pushing them back down, surface. Deeply feel the rage, or the hurt, or the fear, or any of the emotions that surface. Own those emotions by being in touch with them. Don't give them over to blame, self-pity, or martyr. The more honestly you feel these emotions, the more liberated you'll feel.

3. Release these emotions by forgiving yourself and choosing to let them go. Give your Higher Self these negative emotions to transform the negative resonance into a positive resonance of power. Your Higher Self will return the resonance at some point, transformed and healed.

4. Now, open your eyes and engage your reality differently. Be willing for it to be changed, but more importantly, allow yourself to be changed. Choose to challenge the old story and be willing to be new. Start exercising your power of choice. Be different; act differently.

Do these steps each time to separate yourself from the false story. When you do, your life will take on a synchronous fluidity, and the old ways that your unconscious uses to get your attention will be less needed. Always remember to recognize, acknowledge, forgive, and release.

The Cleansing Meditation

Use this meditation to flush away the junk you're holding within you: old psychic contracts, blockages and resistance, negative scripts, fears and anger, etc.

1. Gently close your eyes. Allow yourself to become quiet and still in whatever way you feel comfortable. When you feel calmer, slowly count from seven to one. With each count, feel yourself shifting and changing, both physically and mentally.

2. On the count of one, slowly open your mental eyes. Imagine yourself in your Safe Place. Your Safe Place

should be outdoors in nature, far from the hustle and frenzy of daily activity. Let it be beautiful, enchanting, loving, and filled with blessed solitude. This Safe Place is yours and yours alone. No one can disturb you here. No one can enter this place unless invited.

This place may be a creation of your imagination, a place you'd like to use from a movie or a picture, or a place of beauty and safety you remember from your past. It should not be a building, house, fortress, or castle as these images send the wrong message to your subconscious. The important thing is that you feel safe, protected, and at peace in this haven in nature. Return to the same Safe Place in every meditation. In each meditation, explore a little more of this space; explore each detail. *"Love pays attention to detail."*

3. After you've spent time allowing your senses of sight, sound, touch, taste, and hearing drink in this place, invite your Higher Self to join you. Sit together for a little while. Feel your Higher Self's presence and love. Talk about what's troubling you. Talk about where you'd like healing: mentally, emotionally, physically, etc. *"There's magic in the telling."*

4. Now walk to the edge of your Safe Place. Step across the invisible boundary that separates your Safe Place from the lands beyond. Walk the changing terrain until you come to an enchanted magical grotto. There you'll notice a gentle waterfall cascading down about twenty feet into a clear pool.

5. Remove your shoes and clothes and very slowly enter the pool until you're breast-deep within it. Now, bend your knees and submerge yourself in the water. You'll find yourself able to breathe there. After a little time, stand up once again and exit the pool and walk behind the waterfall.

6. You'll notice a ledge jetting out beneath the cascading waterfall. Walkout and stand fully naked beneath the downpour.

7. Feel the gentle weight of the water as it crashes down around you. After a time, experience the cascading water entering the top of your head and slowing filling you.

8. When you find yourself filled, the water will then flow out of you through the palms of your hands and the soles of your feet.

9. Feel the cascading water racing and cleansing your body and all the organs within you. Sense the water dissolving your blockages and washing away your resistances. Sense the water washing away the negative emotions, and cleansing and healing the areas within you in need of healing. Let yourself get into it. The more you do, the more powerful the meditation.

    Feel the emotions surfacing that need releasing. Feel the darkness and heaviness like clumps of dirt breaking away from you. Sense your limiting beliefs, thoughts, and attitudes like strips of paper dissolving away.

10. When you feel lighter, come out of the cascading waterfall onto the grass by the side of the pool. Close your mental eyes and sense the remaining water flowing out of you through hands and feet.

11. Your Higher Self will now approach you and cocoon you in a white gauze-like robe. Lie robed upon the soft grass, close your mental eyes once again and drift into a gentle slumber. Be very still.

12. When you awake, close your mental eyes once again and mentally count from one to five. On the count of five, open your physical eyes and return to your room. Your meditation is now complete; the magic is now undertaken.

The Parts Meditation

Use this meditation when working with your lesser selves, your Dark Counselors, or whenever you just want work or hang-out with your Higher Self.

1. Gently close your eyes. Allow yourself to become quiet and still in whatever way you feel comfortable. When you feel calmer, slowly count from seven to one. With each count, feel yourself shifting and changing, both physically and mentally.

2. On the count of one, slowly open your mental eyes. Imagine yourself in your Safe Place. Your Safe Place should be outdoors in nature, far from the hustle and frenzy of daily activity. Let it be beautiful, enchanting,

loving, and filled with blessed solitude. This Safe Place is yours and yours alone. No one can disturb you here. No one can enter this place unless invited.

This place may be a creation of your imagination, a place you'd like to use from a movie or a picture, or a place of beauty and safety you remember from your past. It should not be a building, house, fortress, or castle as these images send the wrong message to your subconscious. The important thing is that you feel safe, protected, and at peace in this haven in nature. Return to the same Safe Place in every meditation. In each meditation, explore a little more of this space; explore each detail. *"Love pays attention to detail."*

3. After you've spent time allowing your senses of sight, sound, touch, taste, and hearing drink in this place, invite your Higher Self to join you. Sit together for a little while. Feel your Higher Self's presence and love. Talk about what's troubling you. Talk about your desire to attend to your developing selves. *"There's magic in the telling."*

4. Now invite your younger selves or dark counselors or both to come and join you. Those most in need of your attention will appear before you. Maybe many will come to join you, perhaps only one or two.

5. Who wants to speak with you? Ask. One or two will step forward to talk with you. They may express in words. They may communicate by lashing out at you

in anger, rage, fear, or through other emotions. They may communicate by way of memories from your past. They may express themselves through the feelings you're having. In whatever way they interact with you, listen, and give them your full attention.

Don't debate or argue with them. Just be patient and listen. Let them lash out at you; let them rage at you. Let them cry and weep. Let them express in whatever way is important to them. Your Higher Self is with you; you're safe. They cannot and will not hurt you. All they want is for someone to hear their anguish. Isn't that what you want?

6. When they've expressed themselves, let them know that everything is going to be ok and that no one is going to be left behind. Assure them that you're changing and growing does not mean you're moving away from them or that they're being abandoned and forgotten. Commit to them that you'll heed their calls and respond to their fears. Give them your love; envelop them in your light. It's the desire of your Light and Love that you listen and respond to them, that you love them, not try to fix or correct them. They must heal and grow in their own time and way. All they ask is that you listen and hear their pain, fear, and mournful cries.

Your dark counselors, on the other hand, will try to obstruct and hold you back. They'll use whatever means they can to keep you from your growing. Listen patiently but do not heed their counsel. You drive your car, not them. You author your life, not them. Be patient, forgiving, understanding, and loving. But don't heed their counsel.

7. When you're younger selves and dark counselors finish, thank them for expressing their concerns. Promise them you'll continue responding when needed and reassure them once again that you're not abandoning them. They will then withdraw from your Safe Place.

8. Now let your Higher Self hold you. You may want to cry, get angry, or express other emotions. Do so. Whatever feelings surface, let them come up. When you're ready, and only when you're ready, thank your Higher Self, close your mental eyes, and slowly and mentally count from one to five. On the count of five, open your physical eyes and return to your room. Your meditation is now complete; the magic is undertaken.

Writing down your experiences would be very beneficial, but only if you want to.

Changing Your Self-Image
(The following is a Lazaris technique)

1. Write out the story of your life in approximately 3 to 5 pages. Don't concern yourself with grammar, spelling, etc. You're not writing a memoir, and not sharing it with others. Now read it through from beginning to end once without stopping. If you stop for some reason, re-start at the beginning and read it through once without stopping.

2. When completed, write the story in one paragraph. Now read it through without stopping, one time.

3. When finished, write your story in one sentence. Read it through once.

4. When completed, write your story in one word; this is your image. If you're being honest with yourself, the word will be negative.

5. Now, select another word to become your new image.

6. Write your new story in one sentence. Read it through once.

7. Then write your new story in one paragraph. Read it through once without stopping.

8. Then write your new story in 3 to 5 pages. Read it through once without stopping

Do the process in one sitting. Do not take a break between steps.

Freewriting

A remarkable technique for self-processing and self-healing is an approach called 'Freewriting.'

In her book, *The Artist's Way* (Jeremy P. Tarcher/Putnam Press), author and artist Julia Cameron offers a unique method for awakening creativity called *'The Morning Pages.'* Her exercises have the added benefit of revealing and giving voice to our resistances and obstructions. I recommend this book to all my students.

The various parts of yourself reside in the domain of your unconscious. They express their hurts, fears, resistances, and concerns consciously through the feelings you're having, and in the outer reality you're experiencing.

Everything you observe is an out-picturing of your inner reality. Instead of limiting the voices of your lesser selves to your outer experiences, which is never a good idea, why not give them another avenue of expression. You can accomplish this through the process of Freewriting.

The exercise is simple. Each morning before beginning your day, write no more and no less than three pages of whatever comes up. Don't write about something; just write down whatever randomly appears on the paper. At first, the writing may be slow due to your mind wanting to control the process, but after about two or three days, it'll stop interfering, and the writing will flow more easily. A subconscious and unconscious dialogue will start taking place. Over time you'll get the sense that you're having a conversation with yourself. You are.

Let the writing flow. Don't concern yourself with grammar, legibility, or spelling. Since no one's going to read this, let it come out in whatever way it does.

Freewriting will give your lesser selves, as well as those more real, a more elegant means of getting your attention. But be careful not to control the process. Let the writing flow without interference.

Again don't concern yourself with grammar, legibility, and spelling. Let this activity be free-hand. Never type it on a computer. The act of writing by hand connects you to the neurophysiology of the brain; typing does not.

Freewriting is not journal keeping or diary writing. And you're not writing an autobiography here. Let it be a unique activity. What you write should never be shared with others, even if they're your friends, your therapist, your spouse or partner, or members of your Healing Community or Spiritual Family. When you finish writing, make sure to hide the notebook. Your writing is for you and you alone.

APPENDIX THREE

Glossary

Ancient Ones: The ancient grandmothers (Crones) and grandfathers (Hermits) of times long past. They're highly evolved and are distinguished by having overcome death. Though they still offer guidance and healing through their counsel and love, they no longer walk among us. Yet, if you call upon them with sincerity, integrity, and maturity, they'll respond, often meditatively.

Archetypal Energy: Primal, first cause energy.

Arrogance: Arrogance is the belief that you're better or less than others. It's a means some adopt to mask feelings of shame and insignificance.

Becoming more: Becoming more is the never-ending, ever-evolving process of growing and expanding to become more of who and what you are.

Blame: Blame is the act of placing on oneself or others the source or cause of discomfort as a means to avoid taking responsibility.

Chauvinism: Chauvinism is the distorted perceptions and beliefs caused by the over-predominance of masculine energy. Masculine energy is not male energy, as feminine energy is not female energy. Chauvinism negatively affects both men and women. Because of chauvinism, men fear feminine energy; women distrust it. One of its many voices is the devaluation of imagination (feminine energy) and the over-reliance on logic and reason (masculine energy). *"Fire's hot. Water's wet. What you see is what you get."*

The Chauvinist: The chauvinist is one of the Dark Counselors. It kept you safe when you were younger, or so you thought, by denying or minimizing the power of feminine energy. This distorting energy castrates masculine energy in men and devalues the power of feminine energy in women.

Coming Home: Coming Home is an ineffable state of being where we fully realize our goodness, truth, and beauty, and awaken to our Oneness with ourselves, our Higher Self, our Soul, and God/Goddess/All That Is.

Consensus: The accepted and acceptable views, beliefs, and attitudes held by the vast majority of people.

Constructive Emotion: Constructive emotions are any emotions, positive or negative, you allow yourself to feel: with positive emotions to feel them fully and integrate, with negative emotions to feel them fully and release.

Control: Control is the panic-driven need and action to keep love safe. In so doing, control imprisons the very love it attempts to keep safe.

C.O.R.E: Acronym for conscious, ownership, release, and engage.

Cowardice: Cowardice is the refusal to tell oneself the truth.

Crisis: Chaos that forces compliance and change.

Dark Counselors: The negative ego, the martyr, shame, the dominator (control), the terrorist, the chauvinist.

Denied Dreams and Futures: The refusal to allow yourself a sense of future, goals, dreams, or visions.

Destructive Emotions: Destructive emotions are any emotion, positive or negative, that you'll not allow yourself to feel.

The Dominator: The dominator is one of the Dark Counselors. It was born during your youth as a protector to keep you safe from fear. When you felt frightened and out of control, it encouraged more control and domination from you.

Dread: Dread is the highest frequency of fear. It's the fear that your very being, your very existence, is in jeopardy.

Efforting: Efforting is the effort you put into challenging, fulfilling, and internally rewarding work and activity. It can leave you gloriously tired.

Elegance: Elegance is the ease and effortless flow in the living of life and the fulfillment of desires. It's an evolving process to a state of action where one does less and accomplishes more, and where over time, one does nothing and accomplishes everything.

Fantasias: Fantasias are dreams, hopes, desires that are meant to happen.

Fantasies: Fantasies are dreams, hopes, desires that were never meant to happen.

Free will vs. Determinism: You have free will and free choice in the direction and pacing of your life. What is determined is that you'll someday remember your promise to Come Home, and you'll choose to keep that promise.

Gratitude: Gratitude is a powerful generating energy that elevates one beyond thankfulness and appreciation. Gratitude can lift us to virtuous action and can inspire us to awaken our goodness, truth, and beauty.

Guilt: Guilt is a non-emotion resulting from self-judgment over feeling an emotion you believe you've no right to feel.

Higher Self: Between you and your Soul is your Higher Self. As the name says, it's the higher you. You're a part of your Higher Self, and your Higher Self is a part of you. Your Higher Self is not, and never was, physical. It will, however, take on a physical form to interact with you meditatively. It was your Higher Self who created you and all your many lifetimes. Your Higher Self walks with you always as a guide and companion on your journey Coming Home. And your Higher Self always tells you the truth.

Higher Senses: The higher senses are the senses beyond the five familiar ones: the sense of voice, presence, movement, light, balance.

Hope: Hope is an expectation for a desired outcome. Hope inspires inspiration and is a crucial necessity for dreaming and visioning.

Judgment: Judgment is a fear attempt to distance oneself from the object of judgment.

Lesser Selves: Your lesser selves are your younger, less developed, less conscious selves.

Magic: Magic is the ability to change reality in accordance with one's will, preference, and love.

Manipulation: Manipulation is the act and need to get others to do what you want.

Martyr: Martyr is one of the Dark Counselors. They're the silent sufferers who need an audience to witness their melodrama of being unloved, unappreciated, or overworked.

More Real Selves: Your higher, more conscious selves; your future selves.

Negative Ego: The negative ego is that part of yourself that entered with you at birth. Its function was simply to provide information for your interpretation. But time and time again, it was expected to do the interpreting, a task it was doomed to fail. Over time it came to hate you for this, and now it seeks to destroy you. Your negative ego always lies to you.

Noblization: Noblization is the act of blaming past occurrences for your current actions. *"Because I was hurt so badly in the past, I cannot trust anybody now."*

Parts of Self: Those parts of yourself, past or future, that comprise the totality of you. Though they reside in different times and spaces, they are greatly influenced by your resonance:

by your choices and decisions, thoughts and feelings, and beliefs and attitudes. You go nowhere in becoming more without attending to them. You're no more evolved than the least of you.

Passion: Passion is focused attention.

Passive Aggression: Passive aggression is the act of doing things in such a way as to cause others to become angry at you so you can retreat into self-righteousness.

Pay-offs: Pay-offs are benefits received from a harmful behavior we engage in.

Principles and Character: Principles are the fundamental truths that serve as the foundation of all our beliefs and actions. Character is the act of living your principles.

Projections: Projection is the act of placing onto others your inner images or needs (i.e., projecting father and mother onto other people).

Psychic Contract: A psychic contract is an unconscious bond that ties one person to another living or dead. For example, because your father struggled his whole life "to make ends meet," out of love and honor, you'll unconsciously not allow success to be easy for you. You'll struggle "to make ends meet." Or, because your father expected you to be successful, and because you hated your father, you won't become successful. These bonds are either formed out of love or forged out of hate. All psychic contracts need to be relinquished or re-written.

Rage: Rage is the highest frequency of anger. As a natural human emotion, it has opposing values: Enrage (negative) - a fit of deep and intense anger, highly charged, that gnaws at and tears down an individual over time. Outrage (positive) – an expression of anger, highly charged, that motivates one to change.

Raw Materials: Beliefs and attitudes, thoughts and feelings, choices and decisions.

Resonance: Resonance is a quantum wave and frequency of vibration. All existence, at its essence, functions as a quantum mechanical wave of energy. When two or more waves meet, an independent wave emerges that acts as an attractor. Synergy is an example of wave functioning. A resonance, when interacting with other resonances, can elevate, lower, or compromise its frequency.

Retribution: Retribution is the erroneous belief in karmic or divine punishment for evil deeds or sins committed, real or imagined.

Sacred Hallows: A Sacred Hallow is a place of peace, healing, and renewal found in beauty, enchantment, blessed solitude, and love.

Self-Image: Self-image is who and what you hold yourself to be.

Self-Pity: Self-pity is a non-emotion designed to numb a real emotion.

Shame: Shame is the feeling and belief that you're flawed, defective, broken, or unworthy.

Specialness: Specialness is an ego trap that holds the belief of being better than, or worse than others. Specialness is a form of arrogance.

Spirituality: Spirituality is one's relationship with that which is more than oneself. This relationship includes your Future Self, your Higher Self, your Soul and Spirit, and God/Goddess/All That Is.

The Terrorist: The terrorist is one of the Dark Counselors. During your youth, you tasked it with halting yourself from stepping too far beyond control. Its function was to 'blow-up' your reality and to instill fear so you won't relax your guard. The terrorism we see in the world is an out-picturing of each person's inner terrorist.

Threshold Guardians: Threshold Guardians are archetypal energies that await us on every significant plateau of change and transition. They bring us to fear to keep us from progressing further. But when we address the fear, they'll stand aside and allow us safe passage forward.

Tools of Manifestation: Desire, imagination, and expectancy.

Trust: Trust is having confidence, faith, or hope in someone or something. Trust should never be given blindly.

Validation: Validation is the desperate need to prove you're valid, that you belong.

Victim: A victim is a vocal sufferer who needs an audience to tell his or her dark story.

Vindication: Vindication is the desperate need to correct the wrongs done to you in the past, real or otherwise.

Wholeness: Wholeness is the synergy of all parts of one's self, and their integration into a state of oneness with God/Goddess/All That Is.

APPENDIX FOUR

The American Society of Alternative Therapists (ASAT)

The American Society of Alternative Therapists (ASAT™) is a nonprofit professional and educational association of certified ASAT™ C.O.R.E. Counselors.

ASAT has been certifying ASAT™ C.O.R.E. counselor's since 1990, through its ASAT™ C.O.R.E. Counselor Certification Course, a three-weekend program in both in-house and distant learning formats. Students receive their training by Martin Hart, the C.O.R.E. architect and creator, and upon graduation receive ACC certification.

ASAT's Principal Function

* Train ASAT™ C.O.R.E. counselors.

* Establish state and local ASAT chapters.

* Upgrade professional skills.

* Promote public understanding and acceptance of the ASAT™ C.O.R.E Counseling profession.

* Establish and maintain the guidelines of the ASAT™ C.O.R.E. Counseling practice as well as the ethical and professional standards required for that practice.

ASAT's Objectives, as Stated in its Charter

* To design and conduct certification and degree courses in ASAT™ C.O.R.E. Counseling.

* To design and conduct workshops in ASAT™ C.O.R.E. for the general public.

* To establish, regulate and support state and local ASAT chapters.

* To increase members' knowledge and improve their skills in their work as ASAT™ C.O.R.E. counselors to enhance the quality of service they provide.

* To promote public awareness and acceptance of ASAT™ C.O.R.E. Counseling.

* To improve members skills in the marketing of their services and management of their practice.

* To establish standards by which members guide their professional conduct and practice.

* To monitor legislation, local and national, impacting the field of alternative therapy and to challenge legislation adversely affecting an individual's right to choose or practice non-mainstream counseling.

APPENDIX FIVE

ASAT Training Courses

ASAT™ C.O.R.E. Counselor Certification Course (ACC)

ASAT™ C.O.R.E. Counseling is not for everyone. It's not for those satisfied with merely surviving and getting by or those fearing to take their growth and healing work to deeper levels.

C.O.R.E., an acronym for conscious, ownership, release, and engage, is a guide and a map for those wishing to awaken their unlimited capacity to create their lives consciously and to do so from a place of reclaimed authorship and self-awareness.

Despite what some in the mental health community claim, the vast majority of people do not have issues requiring mental health intervention. A growing number within this vast majority are waking up and responding to the challenge of becoming more, not becoming fixed, or just becoming better. No longer satisfied with merely curing, they seek instead, healing. No longer satisfied with fixing the same old problems, they seek instead to move beyond them; such clients are looking, not for professionals who view their issues as a dysfunction, but as resistances on a journey of becoming more. They're looking for professionals who can point the way to their lost and forgotten capacity to handcraft a life of elegance, enchantment, abundance, magic, artistry, and happiness. They want to live their lives deliberately, not by the whims of fate. To do this, they'll seek out those who can guide them, those who are living such lives, and those with knowledge and skills to help them. They're ready to undertake the guidance offered by ASAT™ C.O.R.E. Counselors.

The American Society of Alternative Therapists (ASAT) has been certifying ASAT™ C.O.R.E. counselor's since 1990, through its ASAT™ C.O.R.E. Counselor Certification Course, a three-weekend program in both live and distant learning formats. Students receive their training from Martin Hart, C.O.R.E.'s architect and creator, and upon graduation receive ACC certification.

Many students take our certification course solely for their own growth and healing; some plan to start a part-time or full-time practice. Some come to us with little or no background in counseling; others wish to gain further knowledge and skills to enhance an already existing practice. All are delighted to find that the knowledge, procedures, and techniques learned in the course not only benefit the lives of those who seek their help and guidance but, more so, their own growth as well.

The Course

Section A (Lessons 1-4)

Before techniques can be taught, students must first understand what impedes a client's healing and growth; what it is that lay at the core of illness and unhappiness. Students gain knowledge and receive the tools necessary to help craft extraordinary lives. In Section A we explore the science of reality-creating and learn the C.O.R.E map essential for its transformation and transcendence. Without processing and programming, no technique will ultimately be successful in affecting healing, growth, and change.

Section B (Lessons 5-8)

Once we've explored the origin and process of illness and unhappiness, and the essential prerequisites for self-healing and authorship, we're ready to learn technique. Section B covers remarkable healing approaches. Each procedure studied affects profound change by releasing destructive beliefs, patterns, and scripts. And they do so more effectively through the processing and programming procedures laid out in the C.O.R.E map, and by exercising the power of their conscious choice.

Section C (Lessons 9-12)

Once we've established the foundation of C.O.R.E. processing and programming, and once we've learned technique, we're ready to put it all together into a structure of practice. Section C teaches students how to conduct counseling sessions and how to establish an ASAT™ C.O.R.E. Counseling practice, as well as how to build that practice successfully.

Doctor In C.O.R.E. Education (D.C.Ed)

Graduates of the ASAT™ C.O.R.E. Counselor Certification Course, who would like to take their knowledge and growth farther, can do so by taking ASAT's doctoral program in C.O.R.E. Education (D.C.Ed). This eighteen-month training program delves more deeply into the C.O.R.E. knowledge and puts greater emphasis on student growth and experience.

Counselors attract clients ready to receive the guidance they require at their various stages of growth. The further along the C.O.R.E. path the counselor travels, the more able he or she will be to guide evolving clients. Counselors not only inspire their clients to more significant growth and success, but they also light the way forward. A Doctor of C.O.R.E. Education marks the map and attracts the clients ready and willing to reach farther in their growing and becoming more, and thus become more successful at the practice.

ASAT™ C.O.R.E. Processing Workshops (ACP)

For those not wanting to become ASAT™ C.O.R.E. Counselors, but would prefer instead to study and apply the C.O.R.E. map for their own growth and learning, ASAT™ C.O.R.E. Processing

Workshops are now available. The course, conducted over a weekend, delves into the C.O.R.E. principles and provides valuable tools and techniques to apply to one's growth and becoming.

For more information on the above courses and workshops, visit ASAT's website at www.asat.org.

About the Author

Martin Hart is author of the books, *The Scented Flowers of Sinjin-Ka* (ASAT Press), *The Magic of the Scented Flowers* (ASAT Press) and co-author, along with Skye Alexander, of *The Best Meditations on the Planet: 100 techniques to Beat Stress, Improve Health, and Create Happiness in Just Minutes a Day* (Fair Winds Press).

Martin is the founder and president of the American Society of Alternative Therapists (ASAT™) and has been in private counseling and alternative health education for more than forty years. Since 1978, Martin has conducted workshops and lectures throughout the United States and internationally on alternative healing and other life-enhancing subjects. He has taught at some of the largest corporations in Asia, as well as top colleges and research facilities. In the late 1980s, Martin combined a series of highly effective healing modalities with his unique counseling approach producing the innovative and remarkably successful healing system *ASAT® C.O.R.E. Counseling*.

As a result of the efficacy of this approach, Martin started training ASAT™ C.O.R.E. Counselors in 1990 to meet the growing number of people seeking this road to greater self-awareness and healing.

Martin still travels the United States and internationally conducting his trainings as well as related lectures and workshops. His courses and seminars have been featured in the Wall Street Journal, The Boston Globe, The London Sunday Telegraph, and other publications. He has also appeared on popular national and international talk radio programs discussing his unique work.

To contact him, and to get more information regarding his trainings and workshops, visit ASAT's website at www.asat.org.

Other Books by Martin Hart

* ***The Scented Flowers of Sinjin-Ka.*** (ASAT Press)

* ***The Magic of the Scented Flowers:*** *Unfolding the healing power of The Scented Flowers of Sinjin-Ka in crafting an elegant and magical life.* (ASAT Press)

* ***The Best Meditations on the Planet:*** *100 techniques to Beat Stress, Improve Health, and Create Happiness in Just Minutes a Day.* By Martin Hart and Skye Alexander (Fair Winds Press)

Books can be purchased in paperback or ebook formats online or in local bookstores. Signed copies can be purchased through ASAT Press (www.asat.org)

www.ingramcontent.com/pod-product-compliance
Lightning Source LLC
Chambersburg PA
CBHW071907290426
44110CB00013B/1314